Praise for *Impact* and Ken McArthur:

"It's great to have somebody that you can turn to and trust. Ken McArthur is somebody that says and does what he says he's going to do. All you have to do is do a Google search on Ken McArthur and you can see the amazing reputation this man has.

—Glenn Dietzel, *AwakenTheAuthorWithin.com*

"Ken McArthur really wants people to succeed and he wants to have an impact on the world and he wants to have an impact on you. He really is one of the most caring people in the Internet marketing industry."

—Dan Kelly, *MiniSiteSecretsRevealed.com*

"We're earning a 7 figure income and it is because of Ken McArthur who really gave us our start and a push in our business."

—Jane Marks, JPE Advertising, *JPEAdvertising.com*

"Ken McArthur is a person who has created a great impact on me personally. He not only walks his talk when it comes to getting noticed and making a difference in people's lives, but he actually has the ability to show other people how to do it for themselves as well."

—Randy Charach, *RandyCharach.com*

"When you're out there you hear about all of these people that are out there getting things done and you don't really know who they are, well he's one of those guys. He's out there, he's connecting, he's making things happen."

—Matt Bacak, *PowerfulPromoter.com*

"Ken McArthur is one of those people that is probably the most powerful person online you've never heard of, unless you're already an online marketer. Ken McArthur is going to go down in history as one of the great teachers that allowed the greatest number of people to become financially free."

—Ben Mack, #1 Best-Selling Author of *Think Two Products Ahead* at *ThinkTwoProductsAhead.com*

"Ken McArthur gives people the ability to believe in themselves and empowers them to actually accomplish something."

—Dr. Ron Capps, the NicheProf, *NicheProf.com*

"Learn everything you can from this Ken McArthur. He's been around for a long time. He's got some great experience and I really consider him a legend in this field and in marketing in general."

—Keith Wellman, *KeithWellman.com*

"Ken McArthur is really just about helping other people with whatever it is that they're looking at doing to succeed."

—Harris Fellman, *SuccessIntensives.com*

"Ken McArthur is one of the most genuinely helpful and sincere persons you're ever going to meet."

—Alex Nghiem, *BackendCashMachine.com*

"I would be without so many great opportunities without having first met Ken."

—Andrew Jackson, Poor Irishman Internet Marketing at *PoorIrishman.com*

"Ken McArthur is a master of sharing the secrets to help you grow your business and in a way that is so sincere and so caring that you just feel like you're his best friend the minute you meet him."

—Tom Beal, *TomBeal.com*

KEN MCARTHUR

IMPACT

HOW TO GET NOTICED, MOTIVATE MILLIONS, AND MAKE A DIFFERENCE IN A NOISY WORLD.

Franklin Lakes, NJ

IMPACT
EDITED BY JODI BRANDON
TYPESET BY EILEEN DOW MUNSON
Cover design by The DesignWorks Group
Printed in the U.S.A. by Book-mart Press

To order this title, please call toll-free 1-800-CAREER-1 (NJ and Canada: 201-848-0310) to order using VISA or MasterCard, or for further information on books from Career Press.

The Career Press, Inc., 3 Tice Road, PO Box 687,
Franklin Lakes, NJ 07417
www.careerpress.com

Library of Congress Cataloging-in-Publication Data
McArthur, Ken, 1950–
    Impact : how to get noticed, motivate millions, and make a difference in a noisy world / by Ken McArthur.
        p. cm.
    Includes index.
    ISBN 978-1-56414-997-8
        1. Success in business. 2. Success. 3. Achievement motivation. 4. Motivation (Psychology) 5. Interpersonal relations. I. Title.
HF5386.M4726 2008
658.4'09--dc22

                                                        2007052891

*This book is dedicated to
my lovely and talented wife,
Roxanne.
Without her support and constant encouragement,
this book would not have been possible.*

Acknowledgments

This book is the result of almost a year of constant research, reflection, and writing. It would not exist without the help of countless people. First, I want to thank my wife, Roxanne, who sacrificed many hours of our precious time together as she encouraged me to complete this work. Without Roxanne, I could never have reached my goal.

My wonderful children, Angela, Melissa, and Stephan, are always there to make me smile and show me the adventure life truly is.

My parents, Irvin and Margaret McArthur, ingrained in every cell of my body that there are no limits on what we can do when we serve others and live it by example. My siblings, Jean, Robert, and John, have been a constant loving, supporting, and inspiring factor in my life since the day they were born—despite the fact that they still believe that I tried to hang at least one of them in my youth.

My mentors and friends are endless. Blake Blakesley, pastor, boss, and friend, taught me how little things can create real impact in the world. Edwin Johnson and Micheal Wert mentored and supported me—and countless others—in the early days at a time when there was no earthly reason for doing so. Together they are constantly proving that decency and quality business practices go hand-in-hand and the results can be amazing.

Frank Sousa and Sterling Valentine, my wonderful friends—best known as the other two famous "three guys on a couch"—are priceless assets to the world and always push me to the next level.

Glenn Dietzel and his entire team mentored me for countless weeks in the writing of this book and the development of my unique position in the marketplace. How wonderful it was to hear his clear message and to grow in my appreciation of the wonderful things he does. Michael Angier, fellow author, friend, and mastermind wizard, taught me the value of a mastermind group and helped me keep my sanity among so many brilliant minds. Mark Joyner, longtime friend, mentor, and brilliant mind, has sharpened my thinking for years now, along with kindred spirits Joel Comm, Mike Filsaime, Tom Beal, Ben Mack, Dave Lakhani, and Rich Schefren—these people are quality all the way.

Brad Semp, another brilliant mind and constant support, helped me to grasp the crucial importance of thinking systemically. Alysan Delaney-Childs taught me how to build a team and volunteered countless hours of her life to make me better.

Rockin' Ronda Del Boccio, the master of Storyation, gave me endless support and encouragement through numerous drafts of raw ideas, while Michelle Alvarez—the rock of my team and the person who gets it all done—held my business together as I wrote. Sid Hale has stood by me from the very beginning. He always is there when I need him and together we make history.

John Willig, my supportive and patient agent, made my publishing dreams come true. Rich Frishman, Jason Oman, Warren Whitlock, and Randy Gilbert, and my excellent publicity team helped me to get my message out to the world.

Finally, my amazing community of friends—the members of *TheImpactFactor.com, jvAlert.com,* and *AffiliateShowcase.com*; the speakers, expert panelists, and attendees at all of the jvAlert Live and "Get Your Product Done" events; and the subscribers of my "Marketing Thoughts" newsletter—has made achieving my dreams possible.

Thank you!

Contents

I f you could make the world a better place for just one human being, would you do it? If you could help solve one of the massive problems facing our planet, would you do it? If you could save one small child, would you do it?

As humans, particularly Americans, we go through living wanting different things—cars, money, love. But at some point in nearly every person's life we want the same thing: to leave a mark, to have an impact on the world around us.

Many people create an impact on someone and often they don't know it. They want that big bang kind of impact, the thing legacies are made of. They want to be remembered for having made a difference.

Which leaves only one problem: They don't know how to do it and yet, anyone can.

Rarely a day goes by when I speak or when I'm traveling around the world that I don't hear someone say, "I'd love to solve that problem, if only I knew how, had the money, or had the time."

And that is where Ken comes in.

Ken's book, the one you are holding in your hands, will show you exactly how you, no matter your station in life at this moment, can have an impact. Read about A.J., or better, read about Muriel Moton. Both are people who experienced tremendous impact on their lives and turned that into impact that transforms the lives of thousands.

And you can too.

Ken has created a road map to show you exactly how to walk through the process of creating impact. He shows you step-by-step what you can do on a day-to-day basis to live a legacy worth leaving. Chapter after chapter, he gives you action items reinforced by real-life examples of people who are doing the things you can do, too. They are living their legacy.

I've often wondered the value of a legacy that you don't experience in the moment.

The really interesting thing about intentional living is that you get to create the life you want, and just creating impact for yourself to create a life worth living, to get what you need, is also necessary. This book will help you do that, too.

In a noisy world, you can be seen. In a cluttered landscape of problems, you can solve one. You simply have to make a decision to do it. There has never been a better time than now for your decision. You can be seen, you can stand out, you can connect with whomever you need to in order to make a difference. And you will if you follow Ken's advice.

The best kind of impact is intentional. You set out to make a difference, and you do. But for who and how many? The answer is: It doesn't matter. Changing one life, saving one life, making the world a better place for my daughter—those are all things that you can do, and, if you follow Ken's plan, you can do it for many, and in a way that is a lot easier and faster than you ever imagined possible.

One of the wonderful things that this book does is show you how to identify impact opportunities. You'll learn exactly how to find problems and solve them. And you'll learn how to create systems to leave behind that allow other people to help even more using your solutions.

In Chapter 4 of the book, you'll learn how to create something that is simple and useful to the people you want to impact. You are trying to make impact too difficult; in fact, the simpler you can make it, the more people can do it, and the more people who benefit from it, the bigger the impact.

As you read this book you'll not only learn to create impact, but you'll be compelled to action. You'll recognize your true potential; you'll discover what it is that you have to give and what legacy you'll leave. You truly can live forever.

This book gives me great hope for the possibility of humanity and for the difference you and I, or any one person, can make if he or she just sets out to do one thing.

Create impact.

I hope you'll take Ken's message to heart and create impact of your own. I hope you'll live a legacy worth leaving. Most importantly, I hope you live the life that is best for you. And, I hope I get to see or experience the result of the decision you make and the action you take today by reading and acting on this powerful message.

I want you to take one action before you go any further. Write down at the bottom of this page the one thing that you'd like to do to create impact and live a legacy. What is the one thing that you'd like to do to make a difference? Write it down now.

I'm happy to thank you now for the difference you are sure to make... and I will.

Thank **you**!

Dave Lakhani
CEO, *BoldApproach.com*
Author of *Subliminal Persuasion:*
Influence and Marketing Secrets They Don't Want You To Know

Y ou are going to make a difference. It will happen even if you do absolutely nothing.

If you do nothing with your child, your child will hurt. Do nothing at work, lose your job, and it won't be you that it affects the most. Your life is bound, in a way that can't be broken, to the people around you. What you do matters.

Give a stranger a smile and he or she may pass it on. In some cases it may make a profound difference to him or her. How badly have you hurt for a kind word at a crucial moment?

So Does a Simple Kindness Make a Difference?

Picture a pool table with the balls neatly racked and waiting for the crack of the cue ball. It's a single ball, and at the most it can only come into contact with a few balls when it makes its first impact.

It's the spread of that powerful impact of a single cue ball that moves the other balls into action. So before you know it, balls are crashing all across the green felt, and you may knock in a ball or two with one whack.

What Kind of Difference Will You Make?

All of the techniques, strategies, and systems in this book can be used for good, and they can be used in some of the most incredibly negative ways that you can imagine. I am trusting that the good will win out. One thing I know for sure: People who can make a positive impact on this world need this knowledge. They need the skills to make sure that the solutions they have to share with the world get noticed and put into action.

I'm Here to Help Make That Happen.

Reading this book will be an intense, "out-of-the-box," productive, results-oriented, fun experience. You'll gain a greater sense of purpose, focus, and direction. You'll develop a specific plan of action. And, you will learn to take specific, consistent action on things that are most important to you—every day.

You are in charge. Bring your biggest personal and professional challenges, opportunities, and dreams. Bring an open mind. Focus. Be ready to take your life, your goals, and your business to the next level of results, joy, and fulfillment.

Here's a Story Guaranteed to Make You Think.

I have two close friends with good hearts who started out much the same.

Both started out in middle-class families with loving parents. Both were intelligent, thoughtful, and generous. Both had developed skills and knowledge that they wanted to share with the world.

Over the years, both friends tried to give back to the world what they could from the talents, skills, and knowledge they gained.

One friend found his efforts rebuffed, his talents unappreciated, and his efforts ignored. For years he kept trying to help others, but, after a while, he became discouraged. Depression set in and he started feeling disillusioned and bitter. Finally, he stopped trying to make a difference.

His young son was trapped in a sea of bitter and angry feelings, and the father passed on his failure to his child. At age 16, the son killed a 5-year-old girl in a drunken accident.

The other friend started out with a simple idea that solved a real problem. Some influential people in the community noticed her idea and spread the word about what she was doing. She inspired the people around her to take action quickly. As her ideas caught on, the systems that she put in place went on to revolutionize an entire industry. Eager crowds of supporters hung on her every word as she led thousands of people to a better life.

What Made the Difference?

Do you ever wonder what causes one person to have such amazing success while others end up in the gutters of life? It's not brainpower, talent, or hard work. It's not that one person wants success more than the other.

The difference is in the knowledge and skills that we have and the actions that we take to use them.

That's Why I Wrote This Book for You.

The whole purpose of this personal impact system is to give its readers knowledge—combined with crucial direction and insight to get your ideas, products, and services noticed, and to motivate millions of people to spread the word about everything that you do.

Why would you want to do that?

Because what you do makes a personal difference in a very noisy world.

This Is a System Unlike Any System You've Ever Seen.

This impact system is unique.

It's the world's only comprehensive impact modeling system focused entirely on making sure that you get your ideas, products, and services to reach millions of people each day. This system drives ideas, products, and services into the public eye every single day, because it delivers knowledge and experience gained through hundreds of case studies and the life experiences of some of the top marketers in the world.

This book reviews a broad range of information of interest and significance to results-minded people. This book reveals not just tactics and strategies, but anything and everything in the fast-moving world of idea propagation and impact development.

This system combines crucial important new ideas of the day with an in-depth personal assessment of your personal abilities, talents, and resources to enable you to create massive personal impact.

Every phase of mass influence is covered. This book contains crucial information on publicity, idea transference, identifying and leveraging networks, motivation, launch tactics, revenue building, automation, and system development.

There is resource after resource inside this book, filled with fascinating and significant stories and information that's useful to you. But, this amazing system doesn't rely on knowledge and information alone. If you have never experienced the effects of this unique system, you can't imagine how useful it can be to you.

It's Crucial That Your Audience Notices Your Ideas, Products, and Services.

The world is a very noisy place, and no one is paying attention to you.

Imagine for a moment that you had to pay attention to everything.

You breathe as your eye scans this page and you feel the air rush past the back of your throat. You hear the whine of an electronic hum from some unknown source. Your neck begins to itch as your collar rubs against the hairs on the back of your neck, and your hands feel slightly cool as they grasp the corner of the page to turn it.

The edge of the page feels slightly sharp, and you notice that as the page turns the shadow of your hand passes across the page and the perceived color of the page darkens, and you wonder why that is. The smell of roses drifts through the room and a light flickers.

Your eye focuses on the letter "Y" and you notice that it is a capital letter, unlike the other four letters in the word. What is that word? Why are there four letters anyway? How many sounds does it take to make up that word? Why did someone choose those sounds? Who were they? When did they live? Where?

If you had to pay attention to everything, you would get nothing done. In fact, you fail to notice most things about your life, and usually that's a good thing. So, every day you notice certain things, and fail to notice others, and your amazing mind has developed a very complicated system for determining what is important to notice and what can be safely ignored.

Are You Blind?

To some degree, you are operating blindly. You have holes in your perceptions, just as the blind spot at the back of your eyeball causes you to have a hole in your vision.

You compensate, much as your eyes compensate. Your brain fills in the gaps automatically and you function as a creature of habit and gut instinct, because you have no choice. There is too much information available for you to be able to process all of the data and come up with the best answer quickly enough.

We make our decisions based on incomplete data, and we act from our instincts and our emotions, and then find the data to justify our decisions precisely because we have no time to judge. Time is the most limited resource that we have.

So how do we make those decisions? Almost instantly!

We Make Instant Decisions at Crucial Moments.

What happens when something is important and has to cut through the maze of overloaded information, glut, and incomplete data, to reach people at a gut level that happens automatically and in an instant?

Imagine that you are standing with your 3-year-old child at the edge of the 50-yard line in a crowd of ten thousand people. It's the championship football game and everyone is focused on the field in the final seconds of the game. The score is tied, and a "Hail Mary" pass heads for the end zone and is bobbling on the fingertips of the receiver when the crowd surges forward to catch a glimpse of the catch.

In the flash of a second, the crowd goes ballistic and people are rushing the field by the thousands. Your eyes travel down your arm to the tightly clasped fingers of your only child and you hear the start of a whimper, but only for a second, as you see nothing but a flash of pink in the roaring mass of trampling feet.

How can you reach such a mass of humanity and tell them to stop when they focus so tightly on the immediate? How will you be noticed when it is important to let people know?

We Already Know How.

It's not a secret.

Hard science is available right now that tells us how we operate, how we decide, and what gets our attention. There are proven ways to get noticed, move the masses, and make a difference in a noisy world when you know the science that makes us tick.

The secret is how to develop a system for systematically putting all that science to work in a way that allows you to optimize the time and resources that you have available to create your own massive, personal impact.

That's Where This Book Can Help.

At least three distinctive types of people will find this book essential reading. Maybe you can find yourself in one or more of these exciting visionary delights.

I call them:

- Missionaries
- Mavens
- Moguls

Do You Seriously Want to Make a Difference?

Maybe you want to change the world, cure cancer, fight poverty, or clean up the environment. What about drive a political message, inspire greatness, share your success, or support the oppressed?

Missionaries take all kinds of forms, but what they have in common is a higher purpose—hopefully one that will make the world a better place.

But, there's a problem. People everywhere need help, and you have solutions to their problems, but the sad truth is that you can't make a positive difference unless you take some positive action. You can't have mass impact if your ideas are never noticed or they don't reach the crucial people that can make them spread.

This Book Will Help You Get Out Your Message.

What's even better, it will teach you how to leverage your assets, skills, and resources—you have them sitting around unused right now—to build your own personal impact system to reach the masses with your ideas, sustain your message, and make a clear difference beyond your own life.

Do You Want to Be a Maven?

Maven is a Yiddish word that describes a person who has special knowledge or experience. Mavens are experts—or at least they want to be—but if you want to be a top-level expert, how can you build the visibility and credibility that you need to rise to the top?

People need the knowledge and skills that you have to make their world a better place, and you have an obligation to make them aware of what you have to offer.

Why Not Be a Mogul?

Revenue is a positive force if you want to make a difference.

I have friends who are wondering where their next meal is coming from, and friends who have made literally millions of dollars, but all of my friends seem to have the same problem:

No Time, No Money

Can you relate to that? Almost everyone can—and that includes my millionaire friends. The hard cold truth is that "No Time, No Money" is an excuse. If you want to be really honest, it's a lie that we all tell ourselves.

Now, before you start writing angry letters, let me explain.

I know that most people have struggles with time and money. Life is not easy, and there is always a shortage of time and money.

Do you think Bill Gates believes he has enough time and money to do all the things he wants to do? Not likely. Try curing AIDS with just a few billion and see how far it gets you.

Isn't life an adventure? Aren't there countless adventures? People to meet, dreams to pursue, things to learn? And most of them take money.

You Get to Choose How to Spend Your Life.

When I was 20 years old, I met a man in his 50s. He had been the successful editor of a magazine, but life took a few hard turns and he found himself divorced, separated by thousands of miles from his kids, and without a job.

His teenage daughter lived with her mother and saw her father only for a week or two during the summer. She idealized him and compared him constantly to her mother, who she was constantly at odds with. Finally, in frustration with her mother and longing for a better life, she traveled across the country and decided to stay with her father.

As it turned out, the reality of living with her father just wasn't what she expected, and before long Dad didn't seem so perfect.

Life with Dad was tough, and finally, out of desperation, her father took a job working as the night desk clerk at a hotel to make ends meet. Despite putting in long hours of work in the wee hours of the morning, the low-paying job still wasn't enough to cover the growing bills, and slowly the father got smaller and smaller in his daughter's eyes.

To add insult to injury, the daughter's boyfriend traveled across the country and slept on the living room couch, paying the father a few extra bucks here and there to help the father make ends meet, until the point that the daughter felt that her boyfriend was actually supporting the family. Then one day...

The father came home with a new throw rug.

And the daughter didn't understand.

How could her father go out and spend $20 on a new rug when her boyfriend was sleeping on the couch to help the family pay the bills?

Her father was in debt and going into the hole even deeper every day, and yet he made the *choice* to spend $20 of his money on a bright, new, shiny throw rug.

I Understand That Feeling.

It would be easy to condemn the father.

He had a family to support and yet he chose to spend money on something that could not possibly make their future more secure.

Was He Wrong?

Maybe *you* know, but I'm very sure I'm not qualified to judge.

I know that life is made up of living, not security. If we do not live, we die, and sometimes when we feel that we should be striving for security, we need to reach for life and dreams.

But, what was the cost of that father having no money?

No Matter What Your Dreams Are, Money Usually Helps.

That's why recurring revenue generation is built deep into the core of this impact system, because if you want to have consistent long-term impact, you need the resources to support your efforts.

You Get to Choose What You Do.

If you have better choices for your time and your money, I applaud you for making the choices that will work best for you!

If you want to create some amazing personal impact, turn the page and let's get started!

1 Person, 1 Sign: Getting Noticed in a Noisy World

Y ou are about to learn how to create your own powerful blueprint for amazing impact, as you capture the world's attention, motivate millions of people to champion your ideas, change lives, and make a real difference in a very noisy world. Can you really impact millions? Absolutely, yes, and it's easier than you think. You don't have to have money, powerful friends, connections, or specialized knowledge. In fact, if you take action on the key principles in this book, you can have those things in abundance, even if you are starting from nothing.

Have you ever done anything small that had a huge impact?

A.J. Velichko did.

Several years ago, A.J. and I were on a youth work trip to help repair some worn-down churches in Boston. A.J. was a natural stand-out in the crowded busload of teenagers spending 10 days of their summer vacation painting, cleaning, repairing, and changing people's lives. He was all boy and full of confidence. A.J.'s biggest desire at the time was to be a male model, and he was very secure in his newfound role. Constantly surrounded by his adoring fans, A.J. lifted the spirits of everyone. Together the kids laughed, A.J. smiled, and I wondered what would become of the amazing A.J.

The older kids in the group were a bit more serious. More experienced, they had been through all of this before. After sleeping on a church floor in sleeping bags with 50 kids to a bathroom and slaving away in the hot, humid summer heat picking up garbage or scrubbing windows, it was natural to want to escape the work. The younger kids would whine and complain as the day went on, but summer after summer the kids grew and their lives changed as they saw the reactions of the people that they met.

You see, the simple actions that the kids were taking didn't seem to be much, but they made a difference in someone's life. Often as they worked, someone would stop and take the time to tell them what a difference they were making. A.J. was watching the older kids, and taking it all in. Although he worked hard that year, he concentrated on his fans at least as much as the much more boring job of slapping paint on the side of a church wall. It was a great trip, and, when A.J. saw the reactions in the faces of the people that he had helped, he changed inside.

The second summer we traveled together to Mississippi to help small towns with hurricane clean-up efforts. It was exactly one year after the disaster of Hurricane Katrina. A.J. was a senior in high school and had come into his own. A natural leader, he set the tone for the entire group as he proved over and over again that he knew the value of the work that he was donating to the forgotten people where the hurricane first hit landfall. In the wasteland of trash left behind by the water and winds, we walked and picked up garbage by the bagful, and the people came out of their houses to thank us. There were dozens of people coming out to thank people for picking up garbage. The gratitude was everywhere. The garbage had been rotting in their streets for a full year and now it was finally gone. It was a simple thing that made their lives better.

A.J. just got it. There was never a doubt in my mind that he knew the meaning of the word *service.* When the next summer came around—even though he was out of high school—I wasn't surprised when A.J. volunteered to be an adult leader for the summer trip to Portland, Maine, to help the homeless. I felt so much respect and pride for A.J. as he planned for college, dreamed of his future with his girlfriend, and set a wonderful example for all of the kids on the trip. The world was so bright. Before it seemed possible, the trip was over and soon after we returned home, a tiny thing happened. It could have been nothing at all, but it turned out to have massive impact.

Try to Imagine What Happened Next.

There's a small spider on a dark night in a moving vehicle. It's not from around here. It was outside, but now it's inside. It could just sit there hidden in a dark space under the seat. It might choose to go anywhere. It chooses to come here. Will it turn right? Will it turn left? It might turn around and never be seen again, but it doesn't. The spider makes a decision that affects thousands of people. Slowly it moves up the doorframe, noticed by no one. It could rest, but the spider moves on. Maybe it's hungry or maybe just curious, but either way it moves higher and higher until it reaches the broad flat expanse of the roof. It hangs upside down in a way that only spiders can do, until it comes to the perfect position and stops.

It could move across the roof and down the opposite door jamb to the floor, but it doesn't. Instead, for the longest while, it does nothing. Maybe it is assessing its choices or maybe it's just thinking about taking a nap, but finally it attaches a thin strand of web to the top of the roof and so slowly you don't even notice it moving, it begins to descend.

Still nothing might be the result of all of this. Spiders come in and out of people's lives all the time without panic and without fear. As long as they stay in the corners unnoticed, humans and spiders live quite well together. It's only when they venture into view that problems begin. Suddenly, the spider speeds its descent and lands squarely positioned in front of A.J.'s eyes as he drives the vehicle along a road in the country on a dark, lonely night.

Maybe if it was darker A.J. would not have noticed. Maybe if he had decided to wait until the spider passed his face then it would have all been different. It seems that the smallest of actions make the biggest impact.

The sudden appearance of the spider hanging in front of his face surprised A.J., and in an instant he made a decision that would change hundreds if not thousands of lives, including his own. He probably didn't think about that tiny decision, because if he had been able to take a moment and consider the consequences of his small action, he would have surely changed his mind. As it was, instinct took over his actions and A.J., for the smallest moment, focused only on the small spider in front of his face.

In that instant the vehicle plunged off of the country road and into a telephone pole, and A.J.'s neck was broken into pieces.

A.J.'s life changed at that moment, but that's just part of the story. I have more to say about that fateful moment and what A.J. did with the rest of his life later in this book. For now it is enough just to remember how one seemingly tiny decision can change your life forever.

That is why this book is so important to you. It's because...

You Make a Difference.

As a teenager, I worried about many things, most of them the usual teenage concerns. Teenagers have more than their share of worries, but I had a few that seemed different—at least to me. One day while taking a shower, I noticed the collection of hair in the shower drain. I started wondering about it, and before I knew what hit me, I was suddenly certain I would be bald in my 30s. I wasn't totally nuts. There was plenty of history. All of my father's brothers were bald. My father had a picture taken at a family reunion showing the tops of all five brothers' heads. They were all gloriously bald except for one head full of black hair: my father's.

Because you are reading this book, I realize that you are smarter than the average bear. That means you may be thinking that people inherit baldness from the mother's side of the family, so let me tell you my mother's father was also bald. My cousins were bald in their 30s and I would think of them, then look down at the shower drain, and see the future coming.

We worry about many things that we don't need to worry about, and I guess I didn't need to worry then. It's been years since I was a teenager and I still have a full head of hair. I don't think it would have mattered much. If I hadn't worried about the hair, I'd have worried about something else. Teenagers always have a lot to worry about, and, for a guy that planned to change the world, I worried a lot. If it wasn't hair it was girls, money, what I was going to do with my life, and the deep, dark, secret thing that I worried about the most: whether I was literally insane. But even with my secret, there was one big worry that topped them all.

Most of all, I worried about whether my life would make any difference at all.

I wanted to make a difference, so I tried a few things. I learned to play a little guitar. I started with simple folk songs, and at first it sounded awful. The strings would rattle and buzz as my fingers struggled to hold the strings firmly against the fret board. Eventually it got a little better. I managed to learn a few simple tunes, but making a song sound similar to the original was tougher. Eventually, I stumbled upon an important musical insight.

> "It's harder to catch me making a mistake if I write the song."
>
> —Ken McArthur

So I wrote songs. You know how passionate teens are. My songs were sad and passionate in a way that only songs written by a teen can be. The first songs were very simple and I kept them to myself. After a while, I got up the courage to share my songs with a few friends. That's when I discovered the amazing power of music to move people's thoughts and souls.

Amazing but true, it turns out that singing simple songs can make a girl cry. Who ever knew? Almost overnight, it seemed, I felt the amazing rush that comes from seeing someone actually listen to what you say. For a teen, that's huge. I saw girls react in a way that made me feel as though I had touched their secret inner core.

But, it wasn't a girl that first taught me about the power of impact. It was a guy, and he was the class president. You know the type: football hero, popular, athletic, smart, the best of the best. Tom was headed for a successful career. In fact, he had recently been selected as a cadet for the Air Force Academy.

One evening Tom heard me singing my songs in the living room of a friend. He just stood quietly in the back of the room listening and not saying much, but something was going on in his head. He must have been thinking, because, as he was leaving, he stopped me and asked me to come outside on the porch. Tom was one of the football guys and I was the music/drama guy, and we weren't close friends, so I was a little surprised. Not shocked, but I wondered what he wanted with me. In the quiet and dark of that old porch, Tom told me. I couldn't have imagined it happening in a million years. What he said took me back a little. On that porch, Tom told me that I had changed his life.

Well, maybe—in a dream world—I did change Tom's life that night, but I think it was the other way around. Tom definitely changed my life. Tom may have forgotten about my song the instant he left, but I never did.

I thought about it a lot. My passionate teenaged brain went into overdrive. What if I had changed his life? What if by writing and singing a simple song I gave him something that he could latch onto as he drove through his already-brilliant career? What if a thought came to him in the middle of a crucial battle in a faraway place? What if the words were spread through his leadership and example?

Tom may or may not have ever thought about that night again. I have no way of knowing for sure. I never saw him after he left for the Academy. But my life was never the same. After that night, I knew. Even the simplest action may be spread until it can never be stopped. It makes no difference whether your actions are good or bad. Either way, your actions will have impact. And that means that I become responsible the moment I begin the viral spread of my actions and words.

The same is true of you. When you do anything that affects another person, you have impact. The question is what kind of impact do you want to have, and how many lives do you want to touch? There are lots of people to touch because...

You're Not Alone.

I know it seems as if you are alone sometimes. You aren't. You don't start out alone or end alone. I know you're thinking about people right now who start out life without parents, or people who die and no one cares. No matter how alone you think you are, you touch someone. If you are born without parents, then someone still has to care for you, and when you die, someone has to clean up the mess. They may not like it, but someone is in this life with you.

Will you do something for me? Start imagining right now who you are going to tell about this book, because it is important—no, it is vital—that someone else know. After all, what can we do alone? How loud can the voice of one person be? How can we possibly make any impact at all with a single voice? We all live and die together, so we might as well have an impact together.

It is in the telling that we grow our impact. It is in the story that we create, the way that it sizzles, fries, and has its own spice-filled, taste-bud-burning explosion. It is in the shock of ice-cold water thrown in the face, in the flash of light and the chest thumping impact of sound that resonates to our very soul.

You cannot have a voice among the masses until you free your small uncertain sound from the confines of self-limiting arrogance. You cannot control; you cannot direct; you cannot manage, but you can impact the world as surely and completely as sacks of weed seed thrown into a farmer's pristine wheat field. The farmer has no choice. No matter what the farmer does, your impact can never be uprooted or controlled or managed, and certainly never be ignored.

Your message can grow and spread, and people can feel your message wherever there is feeling, wherever people gather your ideas can be, and you can influence every thought that can be imagined. And all you need to do is to put your ideas in the minds of others, feed and nurture them as they grow, and make sure that they are given to others as simply and easily as a cold locks into your system after a simple handshake, a hug transmits a feeling, or a pointed glance nails you with reproach.

You Make a Difference.

Your smallest actions have impact even when you don't want them to—even if you choose to do nothing. If you do nothing with your dreams, your dreams will die. If you never let anyone get close to you, then love will turn away. If you do nothing with your money, it will eventually disappear. If you ignore your children, there will be terrible results, and it may last for generations to come. You will influence people by the actions that you take today. Deadly destructive or amazingly uplifting, your life will change the people you meet, know, and love.

From the very day that you are born, you make a difference. Your parents took one look at you and realized that their lives would never be the same. People feel your influence countless times, in amazing ways that you never noticed. Just as the butterfly's wings can change the weather, your tiny movements may create storms that shake the entire earth. Your impact is incredible, and today is the day that you can take charge of it.

What Kind of Impact Are You Making?

You will have an impact, but the real questions are "Will your ideas and solutions be spread to the people that need them?" and "Will your impact make a difference?"

You can have more impact than you ever thought possible, and it's easier than you think. Together we will move step-by-step through simple actions that create massive impact for your ideas, products, and services, and ensure that what you have learned will spread beyond one life.

If you want to have impact, there are key choices that really matter:

- Make right choices, and you can't be ignored.
- Make wrong choices, and you will never be heard in a world that is full of people trying to make their mark.

This book will help you avoid the mistakes and give you influence beyond what you can imagine. Once your personal impact starts to grow, you won't be able to stop it, so start getting ready for success now. You can make a positive difference if you make the right decisions and take the right actions.

Reading this book can change your life forever—literally. I'm going to show you how it happens right now. So take off your shoes and relax for just a minute. Let your imagination loose on the possibilities!

In this media-packed world, it seems impossible to get any message listened to, but imagine that you have a voice that can't be ignored. I'll show you how to get that voice in a minute, but for now just accept the fact that you can have one because...

Impact Starts With a Whisper.

If you want attention, the natural inclination is to yell. Sure, you can yell all you want, but no one is listening. Make the decision to begin your message with a whisper so unique and so compelling that people strain to hear as they move tightly around you. They have to listen closely just to catch the words, and you know you have their attention, because their excitement is growing.

People passing by turn their heads to see what's going on. The room gets very quiet. You pause, and you hear pin-drop silence as people hold their breath. They lean forward in relief as you start again and, when you are finished, they run to spread every unstoppable word. That's impact.

You can't have impact without a compelling story and a unique voice that must be heard. Whether your dream is a successful product launch, a runaway best-seller, or a mission in life, you can give your dream intensity, purpose, story, and momentum, and make it fly! You have a chance to make your vision come true, and it starts today. But first, I need you to do something. This is important...

Mark Down Today's Date in the Margin of This Book.

I'll wait.

Literally—go now—get a pen and write today's date in bold strokes, because I want you to tell me exactly when it happened as you share your success story with me. Today is the day that you make your decision to have massive impact and make a difference. Making this decision will change your life, plus all the lives of people you touch. And you should know when it happened. Years from now, I hope that you will pull out this book and re-read it with a smile, wondering at the amazing life that you have had and looking at that date in the margin—the day everything changed. Too melodramatic for you? I guess we have to...

Overcome the Skepticism of a Skeptical Age.

Think there's no Santa Claus? Put aside your skepticism for a minute. Your dream has already happened.

In 1897, Philip O'Hanlon was asked by his 8-year-old daughter, Virginia, whether Santa Claus really existed. Her friends—you know some of those skeptical types—told her that it was all a lie. Maybe he wasn't so sure himself, or maybe he just didn't want to say, but whatever the reason, Dr. O'Hanlon passed the buck and told her to write to the *New York Sun* newspaper. He told her the paper would tell her the truth.

Newspapers don't always tell the truth.... You know how the world really is. It was a tough time Virginia was living in, too. The editor, Francis Pharcellus Church, was a veteran war correspondent who had reported on the horrors of the Civil War. The world had turned skeptical and had lost faith in much of society, so he saw an opportunity. Church replied to Virginia's question in what became the most reprinted editorial ever run in the English language.

The editorial starts out:

> VIRGINIA, your little friends are wrong. They have been affected by the skepticism of a skeptical age. They do not believe except [what] they see. They think that nothing can be which is not comprehensible by their little minds. All minds, Virginia, whether they be men's or children's, are little. In this great universe of ours man is a mere insect, an ant, in his intellect, as compared with the boundless world about him, as measured by the intelligence capable of grasping the whole of truth and knowledge.

Yes, there is a Santa Claus; he lives in the hearts of everyone who believes in him.

So for all of the Virginias in the world, who are asking if they can really make a difference, let me tell you about a lonely, young man who had a real impact with a cardboard sign. Even though this man had an impact on millions of people, we still don't know his real name to this day. The young man prefers a simple anonymous life, so he calls himself "Juan Mann." Juan Mann is just a play on words, pronounced "one man." So yes, Virginia, "one man" can make a difference. It's already happened.

Can 1 Person Make a Difference?

Juan Mann returned to Australia from living in London, where he had broken up with his fiancée, and seen his parents divorced and his grandmother take ill. Juan's family and friends were scattered across the world, and he was lonely.

One night Juan went out to a party, and something little happened. A stranger came up to him and gave him a hug. No big deal, but somehow, the simple hug made Juan feel as if he were a king. In fact, he felt that the hug was the greatest thing that had ever happened to him. It also gave him an idea.

The idea was a little different. Okay, maybe more than a little different. The idea seemed strange even to Juan, but the idea grew on him. Six months later after getting his hug, Juan decided to fight his loneliness with his idea. He decided to give away hugs to strangers in the mall.

Juan is young, but he isn't crazy. He didn't feel that he could walk up to a stranger without any form of introduction and give him or her a hug, so Juan held up a sign with the words *Free Hugs* printed on both sides. Juan was pretty nervous, but kept holding up his sign and hoped that at least one person would take him up on the offer. For the first 15 minutes no one did.

People stared at him as if he were more than a little crazy. They hurried by, trying not to look him in the eye. Juan started to wonder if his idea was as crazy as it sounded. It went on that way for a while. Finally, a little old lady gave him his first hug, looked him in the eye, and smiled. Something changed.

It's a proven fact that smiles are contagious. After the first hug, more people started to smile and others were encouraged to join in the hugging. As more people smiled, more people were hugged, and soon there were multiple people hugging each other and laughter started to spread throughout the mall. For every person who got a hug, five walked past with a smile on their face. People who had been walking around the mall, feeling lonely and isolated, were connected and laughing, and they felt better. It made a real difference, if only for that moment.

It was good for Juan, too. Soon it was a weekly ritual. Every Thursday afternoon, Juan would leave his job to spend a few hours dispensing hugs in the mall. Apparently, there were lots of lonely people in the mall.

One of the people that took Juan up on his offer of a hug was Shimon Moore. Shimon was a member of a band called Sick Puppies. The band had managed to land a record contract and tour Australia, only to have the record label fold. At that point things weren't going so well.

When money started getting tight, Shimon needed a paying job. Playing with his band at night limited the options, so, for a year and a half, the 20-year-old musician worked odd jobs in his spare time. That's why Shimon put on a sandwich board sign advertising half-price shoes and trudged through Sydney's Pitt Street Mall. Shimon kept the job to fight mounting bills while his band struggled for recognition. Unfortunately, no one was noticing his band, and he hated the part-time jobs.

In September, Shimon put on his sandwich board sign as usual, and, as he walked the mall, he saw Juan dispensing hugs. Something about the smiling people compelled Shimon to go up and give Juan a hug, and he asked him the same question everyone asks him, which is: "Why are you doing this?" Juan gave Shimon the same answer he gives everyone: "Because I like making people smile." Shimon thought it was the coolest idea he had ever heard in his life.

When Shimon met Juan he had just seen Morgan Spurlock's Academy Award–winning film, *Super Size Me.* The film is an exposé of the McDonalds fast food empire. Spurlock put his own body on the line, living on nothing but McDonalds for an entire month, and made a documentary film about the experience. Watching the film inspired Shimon to want to create a film of his own, so the next question was, "What should he film?"

Shimon thought Juan giving away hugs was something that deserved to be documented, and today he says, "If somebody hadn't recorded it, it would have been a crime." Shimon decided to film Juan, and they became friends. Shimon borrowed his father's video camera to shoot footage, and they filmed one day a week for two months. That's when they started getting into trouble with the authorities.

Shimon and Juan decided to take Juan's hugging around to different parts of the city and soon found out that different authorities had different rules. They were not allowed to offer the hugs in some places because the authorities considered them a public liability problem. The authorities thought if anyone got hurt while Juan was hugging someone, the city could be sued, so Shimon and Juan were told that they needed to purchase $25 million worth of public liability insurance.

Purchasing insurance wasn't an option for the two young men, so they decided to start a petition drive to convince the city to allow them to give away free hugs. Shimon filmed the petition drive, and within a few weeks they had collected more than 10,000 signatures. Juan presented the petition to the City of Sydney council, and Juan was allowed to continue giving hugs.

Then nothing much happened, and life moved on.

Shimon's band wanted to move to Los Angeles, California, to get a bigger piece of a bigger pie. Shimon took out a loan from his father, as well as a personal loan. The band's manager lent them some money, and they just kept borrowing money to make it happen. They moved to Los Angeles, lived in a two-bed apartment with four people, and ate pasta and noodles every day. They did a lot of practicing and rehearsing. Nothing had happened with hours of footage that Shimon and Juan had created together.

Juan was still in Sydney when his grandmother died, and he was left to care for his blind grandfather. His head was spinning, and he was alone again while Shimon was busy following his dreams in Los Angeles. Juan called Shimon to tell him about his grandmother's death, and Shimon wanted to do something for him.

That evening, Shimon took a look at the footage that had been sitting useless for months. In a single long night he turned it into a short film accompanied by his own song, "All the Same," which the band had recorded. The next morning Shimon sent it to Juan on a disc as a present with a note that read, "This is who you are."

Spreading Impact

While Shimon was editing the film, the band walked in and suggested putting it up on the video-sharing site *YouTube.com*. He posted it on Friday night. By Sunday, the video had received a quarter-million views.

Once the video reached to a quarter-million views, *YouTube.com* took the video down to make sure the video had clearance from the band. Shimon had to sign a piece of paper giving *YouTube.com* permission to play the video and *YouTube.com* immediately featured the video on their front page. Then the following happened:

- A producer from *Good Morning America* saw the video on *YouTube.com*.

- A television audience of millions watched Juan at work when *Good Morning America* broadcast the video.

- Oprah Winfrey's producer's doctor saw the video, and Juan was invited to appear on her show, *Oprah*. College student Yu Tzu-wei saw the video and started a campaign to "hug everyone in Taiwan."

- "Free Hugs" days were scheduled in Australia, Italy, Canada, the United States, Switzerland, Belgium, England, and Denmark.

- News media featured students from McKendree College giving free hugs before Game Five of the World Series.

- It even spread to China, where a 24-year-old man named "Baigu" was detained by police in Shanghai, after copying the idea, for not having a permit to hold a gathering in a public place.

- The impact grew to influence entire governments.

- In order to combat discrimination against people infected with AIDS and HIV, the French government called on its citizens to embrace strangers who hoisted signs in the street offering free hugs.

That's Impact.

But, people hold up cardboard signs every day. Why did Juan and Shimon have impact when so many other people have very little? I'm going to show you exactly what the crucial differences are and how you can have massive impact on the same scale that Juan and Shimon did.

> "If you want to have a big impact, solve a big problem."
>
> —Ken McArthur

Anyone can get noticed. All you have to do is stand naked in Times Square dressed only in a cowboy hat. But if you want to have a big impact, you have to solve a big problem—or create one. For now, I'm going to assume that you don't want to be the problem, so that means that you need to be looking for problems that need to be solved.

Juan Mann's hugs solved a very real problem. Even in today's connected world, people are isolated. They are often separated from family and friends, and electronic communication is often impersonal and leaves us craving simple physical interactions. Society forces us to be proper and discourages public signs of affection. Juan Mann's hugs gave lonely people permission to connect in a physical way that helped them feel better.

Juan felt the pain of loneliness, and he was offered a solution, but it could have ended there. Juan could have done nothing. Sometimes people just figure out a solution to a problem and keep it a secret. Sometimes they don't share it at all and that can have real impact. Imagine that you discover a cure for the common cold and only use it to fix your own sniffles. Maybe you just share it with a friend.

Juan could have just hugged someone at a party. It might have made that person feel better and may have increased the amount of hugs given out in the world. But, that's not what happened. Juan didn't go to a party; he went to the mall. That choice made a big difference.

Why would Juan choose to go to the mall? Most likely because that's where the people are.

We don't often think of a mall as a community, but it definitely is one. A group of people gathers and shares common interests and resources. Merchants sell goods and people purchase those goods. They may share a common language, a geographical area, an income level, political values, and even loneliness. They are in a "clump."

Where Does Impact Begin?

So the first important action that Juan took was to identify an existing community where people who were lonely were "clumped."

But, identifying that community wouldn't have made any difference at all without more action. The impact that Juan had would have died with a single hug if Juan had never gone to the mall. Even if he had gone to the mall, it would be unlikely that he would have received any hugs without the use of his simple cardboard sign. It was a simple voice that carried through the mall his core message and got him noticed.

Still, Juan's impact would have died if he had given up after the first rejections. People weren't responding because they weren't sure that it was okay to respond. They needed to know that it was safe to hug Juan. Luckily, Juan was persistent and finally had his first hug from a very safe older lady. People saw that it was okay to smile and maybe even grab a hug of their own. As more and more people smiled and hugged, it became easier to join in because it was becoming apparent that people approved.

But, Juan's impact would have died in a single day if he hadn't decided to go back to the mall again. Each time Juan made a trip to the mall, he impacted more people, and he became an identifiable part of the existing community of the mall. By repeating his actions on a regular basis, Juan became a respected part of that community and developed relationships that would grow the impact that he had and ensure that his dreams wouldn't die.

Shimon was a key part of the mall community, and he brought some important new elements that would eventually increase the visibility and impact of Juan's hugs. By capturing the feelings and emotions of people in the mall community and Juan's impact on video, Shimon was able to transfer the impact of the moment in a format that could be spread to millions of people.

If Shimon had never filmed the moment, Juan's impact would have been limited to a small mall community in Australia. As it turned out, the filming of the event focused attention on the event even in the moment as it was being filmed.

Shimon and Juan identified other places where people gathered and expanded into more communities. Hugging was spread into places that had never seen Juan giving out hugs. As each new location was added, the impact grew.

As a result of this growth, more attention was focused on Juan, and eventually that attention created controversy as local authorities began to worry about the impact that Juan's hugs were having throughout the city. Adding controversy to an event can be likened to throwing gasoline on a fire, and, if you throw enough on, you will definitely attract attention. The flames of controversy attracted key members of two more communities— the local government and local media—who spread the news through the entire city.

Key Influencers

Let's admit the fact: There are key people in every community. Those people can make sure that your ideas and solutions spread quickly through the group that they influence. In some cases, these groups are massive. As the local government and local media began to notice what was going on, key people within these groups started to spread the message through their influence.

Juan Mann had an emotional story to tell. As the controversy increased, key influencers repeated that story to more and more people. The intensity grew as Shimon and Juan leveraged their existing relationships with people touched by their efforts. They created increasing social proof that their actions were appropriate and desired. Their efforts were rewarded with an official approval from the city. Juan and Shimon had made a big impact on a city.

And then it all died down and might have gone completely away. The video sat unused, the controversy was over, the local media and the local government stopped talking about Juan, Shimon headed off for Los Angeles, and things went back to normal.

That all changed when Shimon, in a single night, edited the video, added the unimaginable power of music to the visual impact of Juan at work changing lives, and introduced it to a larger community called *YouTube*.

This Is a Noisy World.

More than $5 billion are spent every year on media buys in the United States alone by people who are trying to get noticed. We are exposed to countless messages every moment of our lives. Within sight of my desk, I can count hundreds of commercial messages. That doesn't even include the countless people, non-profit, and religious organizations that are trying to grab a piece of my mind, my heart, and even my soul.

How many people do you know right now who are on a personal mission? Maybe you are someone who is blessed—or cursed—with a dream of your own. You may feel as though you are screaming at the top of your lungs, and still people aren't listening, don't notice, and don't seem to care.

The ambient noise is just too great. There are too many demands on our attention. There are too many opportunities to follow them all. There are too many wonderful ideas and no time to enjoy most of them.

How Do You Increase Your Impact?

So how can one person make any difference in this noisy world?

- How can you get your ideas noticed?
- How can you motivate other people to spread your ideas?
- How can you get the maximum impact for the least investment of time and resources?
- How can you sustain your impact over time?
- How can you get exponential impact with simple choices?

- How can you identify key people and spheres of influence to target?
- How can you persuade other people to help?
- How can you leverage existing networks and media?

□ □ □

This book helps you identify the leverage that you already have and practically forces you to take clear actions that will result in amazing impact for anything that you want to dream. There are choices you will make that will make a huge difference in whether you are noticed or ignored.

Join the adventure as together we discover:

- How to get noticed in a world that doesn't want to listen to you.
- How to find your audience and make them your advocates.
- How to take simple core actions that create massive impact.
- How to identify existing networks that want what you have.
- How to target key influencers that can make it happen right now.
- How to convince key partners to share their customers and reputation.
- How to use automated systems to spread the news even faster.
- How technology explodes your impact.
- How to generate recurring income for all of your projects.
- How to motivate millions to action based on over 100 years of scientific research.
- How to make your impact live beyond one life.
- How to make a real difference in the world, one person at a time.
- And much more.

Along the way, I'm going to share some stories of people who have changed millions of lives with their impact and let you in on key choices that made the difference. Imagine getting the behind-the-scenes stories directly from people including Craig Newmark, who *Time* magazine listed as one of the most influential people in the world. Or meet Matt Mullenweg, the creator of *WordPress,* who is listed at the very top of lists of the most influential people in the technology revolution.

Not all of our impact case studies will be names that you recognize, but all are creating their own personal impact on the world. Either way, you will soon know their story and their secrets. This is not theory. This is impact in action.

Your 1st Gift

There are reasons that key people capture the attention and respect of the masses while others pass by without a trace. Anyone can yell, make noise, and get noticed. Fame is easy, but to have real impact you need a personal blueprint that makes sure that you don't miss a single opportunity.

One opportunity can change your life and the lives of millions of people that you touch.

The first step is to figure out exactly where you are right now. After all, every person is different. We all bring specific talents, interests, resources, skills, knowledge, and aptitudes that we can leverage to maximum effect. As we grow and learn, we constantly refine our experiences, develop new resources, and grow our impact by building key relationships.

To help you identify your key assets and help you figure out what strengths you have at this instant, I've created the "Impact Assessment Tool." You will be using this tool throughout the remainder of this book to build your own personal system for creating impact. Find out what you bring to the table right now at *TheImpactFactor.com/resources/.*

So what happened to A.J. Velichko?

I have so much to tell you. The lessons that A.J. and so many others taught me are spread throughout my life, and their stories fill this book. Together we are going to build a personal system for you that will amaze you and impact millions, but the heart of this story is not in a system. The heart of this story is in the lifeblood of the people who have impacted our lives and the people who will be touched by us as we live our lives. Every person who reads this book will impact someone. As of this instant, you are part of a family, and together we will create impact far beyond one life.

Turn the page for the rest of the story.

Your Personal Impact Action Plan

L et's get going! You can start building your own personal impact system by taking a good, long look at yourself.

What Do You Bring to the Table?

You have unique skills and experiences—building blocks that you can use to create amazing impact. Your goals are unique, even if they aren't entirely clear yet. Put together, your skills, resources, and goals can provide you with the purpose and system that you need to take your impact beyond your imagination.

To help you take the first step in this adventure, I've developed a free Impact Assessment Tool, which you can use to create your personal impact profile. This unique tool will help you learn more about your skills, resources, and goals than you ever thought possible. When you use this one-of-a-kind tool, you will clearly identify resources that you already have, create a clear focus using your current skill sets, and discover many new skills that you can develop to increase your impact. As you focus both your business and personal goals, you will be able to create an action plan that will systematically set you on the optimal path to incredible success.

I want to urge you to take the time to use this powerful tool to discover your own personal path for creating amazing impact. It will give you some wonderful insights into the unlimited possibilities for your personal future. You can find the Impact Assessment Tool online right now at *TheImpactFactor.com/resources/*.

CHAPTER 2

What Motivates You?

Every person is destined to create his or her own unique impact. The reasons that we want to touch the world are as individual as the ways we affect other people. Start by asking yourself what really drives you. Do you want to be famous? Do you want other people's respect? Are you looking for financial security, or do you really want to be extremely wealthy? Are you on a personal mission to change things that you don't like? Are you trying to right a wrong that exists right now in this world or are you trying to prevent a disaster?

All of these motivations can create massive amounts of impact for good in the world—and equal amounts of evil. There will be days and nights that you wish you had never taken action, and you will need all the motivation you can drag out of your soul, so now is the time to find out what will be most likely to get you through those times. Clearly, the first step is to determine what makes you tick. What gets you out of bed in the middle of the night with your heart pounding to take action?

Ask yourself now whether you would rather have fame or wealth, security or adventure, purpose or freedom. You may be able to have it all, but the hard cold fact is that you will often have to choose in a matter of seconds between two things that you hold very dear. Before you reach that crucial moment, I pray that you will have thought about the questions and make the best choice that you can in time to live another day.

About Those Value Judgments

I won't make value judgments on you or your actions. I am unqualified to judge the reasons that you do what you do. Many people who have been motivated by reasons that others find selfish or shallow have created massive impact for good. Many people trying to do good things have caused horrible things to happen. All motivations are destructive when driven to extremes. How many people have started on noble missions only to find they are broken and desperate? Desperation can drive people to actions that destroy the mission that they live for and hope to build and grow.

No matter how saintly your mission in life starts, you should always be aware that growing impact demands ever-increasing responsibility. You need to be aware of what works when it comes to motivating yourself, because you are going to need massive amounts of motivation to reach your full potential. Life doesn't come easy, and, if it comes easy to you, then you aren't reaching your maximum potential. Start stretching a little.

All I'm asking is that you be honest with yourself, even if you don't share that honesty with me. Some of us don't like the things that motivate us. Even if we do, we aren't always eager to let the world know exactly what they are.

What About Your Ego?

As much as I hate to admit it, there is more than a little ego involved in my wanting to have a great impact on the world. If there wasn't, then I might not work quite so hard to make it happen. I find energy in the approval of crowds of people that share my vision and magic in the changing of lives and the sight of growing numbers of people passing on my vision to other people. I love the feeling of capturing a moment of intensity and passion. I want to feel a room of people surge with the strength of my convictions and sense the heart of a room enveloping everyone within the sound of my voice. I love the moment. It drives me each time to extend it and make it bigger.

Those kinds of moments won't motivate everyone. Some people hate being the center of attention. They build in the background. They support rather than lead. They create better than promote, or implement rather than innovate. Whoever you are, you need to know what drives you to be your very best—even if you don't want to share your secret with the world. Facts are facts, and saying that they aren't won't change them.

> "If chocolate motivates you, eating all the spinach in the world is not going to help you get things done."
>
> —Ken McArthur

The Magic Motivators

A combination of three things—fame, finances, and mission—motivates most people who want to have an impact. Spend a few minutes and honestly think about which of the three elements motivates you and to what degree. Maybe you don't want to be famous or wealthy at all. Maybe your sole interest is to change the world. Maybe your heart yearns for the recognition that you feel rightly belongs to the words that you have to share with the world. Maybe you want to be secure financially, or maybe you want to have the riches of Bill Gates and the power to support countless causes beyond your ability to imagine.

If you want to reach your maximum potential, all three elements will be a part of your personal impact system. The mysteries of curing cancer can't be discovered without money to fund research. Mother Teresa wouldn't have been as effective without being well known, and, if you don't do something worthwhile, all the riches and glory in the world are useless. Given the fact that you need some degree of all three, start figuring out what motivates you right now and what seem to be your greatest strengths. You can start there and build forever.

The Impact Assessment Tool will help you move through a series of questions to help you define your motivations, your resources, and your skills. It will help you define your goals and match them to the next steps you need to take right now to kick-start your impact and get the gears in motion for unbelievable results.

Start thinking right now about what your life purpose or mission might be. What do you value most in life? What needs to happen so that you can feel that you are honoring your values?

A Note From Jack Canfield

I love to read. As a teenager, I spent much of my summers making a daily trip to the library, and each day I collected a stack of books that I would hungrily devour and return the next day. At the time, my tastes leaned toward science fiction and biographies. Later I expanded my interests, but I'd really never read books that focused on personal success until Jack Canfield sent me a personally autographed copy of his new book, *Success Principles.*

I knew right away that Jack Canfield had no idea who I was. He was, after all, the co-creator of the *Chicken Soup for the Soul* series and had developed 40 *New York Times* best-sellers, including 11 that went to #1. Jack is one of the driving forces behind the development and delivery of more than 100 million books sold through the *Chicken Soup for the Soul* franchise, which *Time* magazine called the "publishing phenomenon of the decade" (June 8, 1998).

Jack runs a billion-dollar empire that includes licensing, merchandising, and publishing activities around the globe, and writes a nationally syndicated newspaper column for 150 papers worldwide, not to mention that

Jack holds two *Guinness Book* World Records. One is for having seven books simultaneously on the *New York Times* best-seller list—beating out Stephen King—and another for the largest book-signing ever.

That doesn't even mention his appearances on shows and networks including *Oprah, 20/20, Inside Edition, The Today Show, Larry King Live, Fox and Friends, The CBS Evening News, The NBC Nightly News, Eye to Eye,* CNN's *Talk Back Live!,* PBS, QVC, and many others. Talk about impact. Jack has touched the hearts and minds of millions of people.

Still, how can you get a personal note from someone of such importance and not read his book? Jack Canfield had personally written a note asking me to promote his new book, so I read it. Then something amazing happened as I read what Jack had written. On page 22, Jack asked me to take the time to complete an exercise.

Please know that I am that contrary person in the back of the room at a seminar who typically refuses to follow instructions. If the speaker tells me to write it down, I lose my pen. If they tell me to stand up, I tend to quietly move to the back wall and watch the rest of the attendees going through the motions. If they tell me to shout out slogans, I tend to mumble.

Getting Your Life Purpose on Paper

Completing the exercise was extraordinary. I followed Jack's instructions and answered four simple questions on page 23 called "The Life Purpose Exercise." Jack made me stop and think for the first time in years—actually decades—about what was important to me. The impact was unimaginable. If Jack hadn't led me to that moment, my life would have been much different, because I probably wouldn't have taken the time for the next several decades to think about what was important. By then, decades would have been lost and countless opportunities missed.

Right now, you have a chance to think about your own purpose and your own life goals. Life doesn't have to be a survival exercise. You are achieving goals every day. Those goals might as well be the important ones. You can't focus on the important goals if you don't know which ones they are. Figuring out which goals are important isn't always easy, but if you focus first on why you are doing what you are doing, it will soon be very clear for you.

The purpose of Jack's exercise is to help you define your purpose in life. By the end of the exercise, I had defined mine. You may be thinking that you don't have a purpose or that you don't have a clue what that purpose would be. You may even feel trapped about putting down a single purpose in life statement. Don't worry. Your purpose in life will constantly change, grow, and take on entirely new dimensions; mine certainly did. You just need to start somewhere.

Living a Decent Life

Here's what I wrote at the time:

Purpose in Life: *"To make a decent living while helping as many people as I possibly can achieve their own goals for a quality life."*

Over the years, my purpose in life has grown and changed, and it will continue to grow and change as I achieve some goals and abandon others. Today I focus on helping as many people as I possibly can to achieve their own goals for making a real difference in the world, but let's look at my first attempt.

I had to take action on that fateful day, and today you need to start from the place you are living, thinking, and dreaming right now. By the way, I still want you to be able to make a decent living—how can you have massive impact if you can't put food on the table? Here's what I was thinking at the time.

In achieving my goal, I wanted to remember three things:

1. Decent
2. Helping
3. Quality Life

Decent is an interesting word. There are several meanings, and I purposely used that word because it covers several things at once.

Definition of *Decent*

- ☐ Characterized by conformity to recognized standards of propriety or morality.
- ☐ Free from indelicacy; modest.
- ☐ Meeting accepted standards; adequate: *a decent salary.*
- ☐ Morally upright; respectable.
- ☐ Kind or obliging: *very decent of them to lend you money.*
- ☐ *Informal.* Properly or modestly dressed.

I want you to know that you can make a decent living.

What's more, I want to show you how you can make a decent living and still maintain your scruples, keep your ego in check, and still be able to face your significant others without shame when you walk in the door. I want you to be able to walk into your church, synagogue, mosque, or parent's or best friend's house and still be able to hold your head high, and be proud of what you have done and how you make your decent living.

This is not about how you can make a million dollars—although, if you do make a million dollars or more using these principles, please let me know—and it's not about anything easy. Life is hard. Anyone want to argue that one? I didn't think so.

Easy Money

I recently made more than $5,000 in one month by putting up one little piece of HTML code on a Website. Was it easy? Sure. It took me less than five minutes. Okay, I didn't count the four years that I spent building up the site that I put the code on. Of course, I didn't count all of the countless things that I tried that didn't make me a penny either.

Was it decent? Whew, that's a harder question. Any time you make a bunch of money with "little" effort, it makes a person who is trying to be decent stop and think. In this case, it was advertising income. I placed some Google AdSense code on one of my sites, and Google paid me a good chunk of change for displaying their ads. That sounds ethical, but maybe the content of those ads didn't make the world a better place. On the other hand, maybe people clicked on those ads and found the perfect tools for making their life better.

To be honest, I don't really know whether the world is better because of those ads, but it's something that I want to think about. In fact, I *have* to think about it if I want to meet my objectives because of that pesky little *decent* word in my goal, and that troublesome phrase *helping as many people as I possibly can achieve their own goals for a quality life* that snuck in there somehow.

Taking Action

If step one was setting my goal, starting now—sitting in my basement— how do I achieve my goal?

Clearly, I need to take action.

Jack Canfield developed what he calls the "Rule of 5" to meet his goal of getting *Chicken Soup for the Soul* to the top of the *New York Times* best-seller list. Jack's "Rule of 5" requires that every day Jack do five specific things to move his goal to completion.

Completing five things each day doesn't sound overwhelming, but imagine this:

- Five pages of writing a day equals seven 250-page books in a year.
- Five new customers a day equals 1,825 customers in a year.

The list could go on forever, but you get the idea. By the way, Jack met his goal. *Chicken Soup for the Soul* eventually sold more than 8 million copies in 39 languages. How did he do it? He did five things a day. Maybe it was five interviews or five press releases or giving away five review copies. Jack did whatever he could as long as he did at least five specific things every day to move closer to his goal.

The Number-1 Problem

What is the number one problem for people who want to earn a decent living? The biggest problem is that most people read, study, think, dream, plan, and then...do nothing. The number-one problem is failing to take action in a meaningful way. And there's something even more important before you take action...

Action Step: Do at Least 5 Specific Things Each Day to Move Closer to Your Goal.

So, what am I going to do today to get closer to my goal?

What you do will be different from what I do, but let me make a couple suggestions for today.

1. Set a goal.
2. Take action on five specific things to move you towards your goal.

How to Set a Goal

Decide what you want out of life. Here's an obvious statement that we rarely consider:

> "You will be much happier if you spend your life doing what you want to do, instead of what you don't want to do."
>
> —Ken McArthur

When the chips are down and you just "have" to work harder because you have absolutely no choice, what do you want to be doing?

Mark Joyner, best-selling author of *Simpleology: The Simple Science of Getting What You Want*, uses two examples—sex and picking up dog poop—when he talks about deciding what you want to do. So what do you want to be doing: having sex or picking up dog poop? For the record, most people choose sex over picking up dog poop. Maybe those two options are extremes, but the truth is still there. You get to choose how you spend your time.

I can hear you now: "The heck I do!" or some stronger language depending on your linguistic preferences. If you're honest, you know it's true. Maybe you don't control everything in your life, but you do have choices even though those choices have consequences.

You're Not a Toddler Anymore.

If you don't like your spouse, significant other, parents, or roommate, you can move out. If you don't like your boss or your job, you can quit. Will you pay for it? Absolutely, but you get to choose.

Let yourself dream for a bit, and imagine that you are a toddler. You have everything that you need. You have food, warmth, shelter, and love, and you can express yourself any way that you like. If you don't like the food, you can spit it out. If you aren't happy, you can scream at the top of your lungs. You have no fear, and, if you want something, you head straight for it without even thinking for a second about the consequences. You didn't know kids had it so good, did you?

Then as you get older, people start telling you to stay away from things, stop crying, and grow up! That's when other people start imposing their dreams on you:

- You can't do that!
- Why don't you think about someone else?

- Slow down!
- Stop that!
- Get a good job!

This is followed by:

- You should really....
- Why don't you...?
- You'd be a better person if you only....
- I really wish you would....
- Why can't you...?

It's Time for Your Dream List.

If you really want to get what you want out of life, you need to refocus your thoughts and get rid of all of those tendencies to fulfill other people's dreams.

It's okay to have your own dreams. Make a list of 100 of *your* dreams. Yes, I'm talking about an actual written list. At first, it will be easy, but eventually it gets a little tougher. Don't put any value judgment on your dreams. It doesn't matter if these are *good* dreams. They are your dreams. Think of it as an "I Want" list. When you get down to "I really want to stop writing this list," you can quit.

After you have your list, scan through it and start asking the question: "Why is this on my list?" Many things on your list may have almost nothing to do with what you really want. One rule of human nature is that we are sidetracked, trying to pursue things that are unrelated to our goals to get to what we really want.

> "Go straight for what you want, not the things that you think you need to get there."
>
> —Ken McArthur

Okay. Now you have a list and you've done some thinking about why these dreams are on your list. Scratch off any that aren't the real goals in your life.

Here are two obvious examples that you already know:

- Money does not equal happiness.
- Marriage does not equal love.

So, if your real goal is happiness, don't put down "Make one million dollars." And if your real goal is being loved, don't put down "Get married." Your list is your own. Don't put my dreams in your list.

Here are some areas to consider:

- Artistic
- Career
- Education
- Family
- Financial
- Health
- Pleasure
- Public Service
- Religious

> "Dream about what you want to give."
>
> —Ken McArthur

When you start making your list, you may be tempted to dream about things you can get, but also think about what you can give. There is no greater reward than giving. You don't have to wait until you have met all of your other goals before you start giving. Now all you have to do is condense your real dreams into concise goals and take five specific actions to move you closer to your goal.

Goals Should Change Constantly.

Over time, my purpose in life has changed. The scope of what I am doing right now is beyond my original goal of helping people earn a decent living. Now I am trying to help people make a positive impact, change lives, and make a difference in the world. If your goals aren't changing, then you aren't growing, so make sure that you take the time to refine, replace, and revise your goals constantly. You can always make them better than they are today.

This morning, I walked down the two flights of stairs to the basement and went straight to the e-mail. I make this mistake often. Even though much of my business is e-mail-based, e-mail can keep you from producing results. I love good e-mails. Here are a couple of the comments that I got today when I collected more than a thousand e-mails this morning:

"Excellent! Gold star, A+. All those good things."

—Jackie

"All I can say is brilliantly refreshing and refreshingly brilliant."

—Tony

These kinds of messages can make you feel great, gold star, even brilliant, but don't get too caught up in believing your own press or even the comments of a few of your friends and customers. There's always somebody waiting to bust your bubble. Take the good stuff with a grain of salt, enjoy it, and use positive comments as testimonials in your marketing, but, when you get something negative, take it with a truckload of salt. I'd give you an example of some of the hate mail that I get, but I try to delete it as soon as possible, because...

We Become What Other People Tell Us We Are.

Now that's a scary thought. The problem is that it's true. If enough people tell us how awful we are, then we come to believe it. So what's the cure?

> "Surround yourself with positive, successful people."
>
> —Ken McArthur

I can't emphasize this enough. If you have a negative spouse, boss, or friends, and you just can't bring yourself to get rid of them, find a bunch of people who are cheerful, positive, and happy to hang around with and spend the majority of your time with them. If you don't, you die on the vine.

Getting Started

When I first started my Internet business, I talked to the pastor of my church. No, I wasn't looking for spiritual advice. I was looking for people. Frankly, I had a big problem.

I was sitting at my desk moments before I got my freedom. My mind wandered back across my life, and I was scared and excited in the same breath. I had moved reluctantly into my 50s knowing that I found my "Peter Principle" level. I had finally risen to the level of my incompetence.

For the last few years I'd been a software developer for a small company that wrote forecasting and logistical software for Pepsi all over the world. Pepsi had been using this tiny company for the last 10 years to create the systems that made sure that cans and bottles of Pepsi were distributed in a way that made sure that just enough Pepsi, in just the right packaging, was delivered with the least amount of freight possible. It was important work. After all, freight cost was a huge percentage of the total cost of a can of Pepsi, and our software could predict better than any single human exactly what products Pepsi should produce, how much, and when it should be delivered from what location.

The software hadn't changed much over the years. The core of the system was 10 years old, developed for the DOS operating system, and the world was moving to Windows. It was now officially an antique, even though it had been updated constantly for years.

I love learning and trying new things, so I was put in charge of developing a new version of the software that would take advantage of all of the new features of the operating system and save our contract with Pepsi. It was a heady, exciting time as I helped to move the company into the future. There was the amazing experience of creation of the new interface. Then there was the tense thrill of presenting the software to the executives of a Fortune 100 company. There was hope and excitement in the air as we waited to hear what Pepsi had to say about our work.

Pepsi told us that the software system looked great, and then decided to...wait.

Suddenly the work was done and the future was very uncertain. I knew that Pepsi was talking with Oracle and HP, among other giant software development companies. The small company that I worked for only had three programmers. Pepsi didn't say "yes" and they didn't say "no." They waited, and after a while the future didn't only seem uncertain, it started to feel bleak.

The company that I worked for was a one-customer company. Oh sure, we had a few other clients. We sold our software to some tea companies and Dr. Pepper, but if you really looked at the sales numbers, we had one customer—Pepsi—and they were waiting.

I was in my 50s and making the best salary that I'd ever made in the most important position that I'd ever held. In many ways, I felt on top of the world. I enjoyed being the only programmer in the company that really understood the power of the new system. I loved taking something from scratch and building it into world-class software. It was inspiring, it was fun, and, before it seemed possible, we finished the software.

It was done—or maybe it was me. I needed that healthy salary to live in one of the nicer suburbs of Philadelphia. My daughters were headed to college, finances were tight, and my skills were starting to feel a little dated. As much as I wanted to learn new things, I couldn't seem to keep up with the pace of a steady stream of young people, fresh out of spending the last four years studying the "new stuff" full-time, while I spent my time building new systems.

I knew that I had them beat in experience, but my boss could hire a fresh college graduate for a fourth of my monthly expenses, and I was nervous thinking the boss would soon figure out that fact. We had almost finished the software, and I knew that the next 10 years would be spent polishing and fine-tuning even if we did get the contract.

I was looking for freedom, but there were a few obstacles.

Picture this:

I'm working at a well-paying job, but life is not secure at all. The company that I'm working for has one big client and that client is going to *think*—for the next six months—about renewing their contract. Ever been in a job that wasn't totally secure?

Well, there's more. I'm getting up towards that wonderful "golden age" of my business career. That means that I was earning at the top of my earning potential, but who would you hire?

- A rapidly aging guy who wants enough money to support a wife and three kids—two of whom are headed for college soon, and you know how much that costs.

- A bright 20-something who just spent the last four years of his life devoted to learning the latest and greatest new things, and who will work for a quarter of what that rapidly aging person needs.

I start thinking about the Internet. I think I want my own online business. In fact, I really like that picture—no commute, no boss, lots of freedom, and easy cash. Oh yeah, and by the way, I have a very realistic wife. She's not totally convinced. In fact, let's just say she is downright skeptical. You see, she has known me for more than 25 years now and she has managed to figure out every single flaw that this old man has.

You know all of those tests that people give you to say whether you are the business owner type? Let's just say that I had to fudge a few answers to get a passing score. Come on—admit it: Someone has at least hinted at the idea that you can't achieve your goals in life. It happens to everyone. It certainly happened to me.

It turns out that it is much easier to convince people that you are a failure than to convince them that you will be a success. All I need to do is convince someone important to me that I am completely unemployable—not so hard to do. After I spend a few months convincing my wife that I'll never be able to get a job again, we come to an understanding.

I can go into business if:

- I don't spend a dime on the business.
- I don't go into debt.
- I don't make anything less than I am at the current job.
- I make sure my income *never* goes below my current income level.

Okay, sounds like a plan to me.

Don't Even Hint That This Is a Good Way to Go Into Business.

My first thought was, "She's absolutely right, I have to be completely nuts to go into business." My second thought was, "I need to talk to Blake."

Let me tell you a little about Blake Blakesley. Blake has a number of roles in my life, but, before anything else, Blake is a friend. We met about 12 years ago when Blake became the pastor of the church that I attend. I still remember the first time that I talked with him in his office shortly after his arrival. Blake is about my age. We shared an interest in music and love of movies. We talked easily together and our attitudes and love of people were similar. Blake seemed like a person I would like to get to know—as a person, not just as a pastor.

Maybe I spoke up because I was the son of a minister and knew a little about the demands that a congregation could make on a new pastor. Maybe it was just my personal interest in Blake the person, but something at the time prompted me to say, "If you need a friend, I'm available." Blake looked at me a bit strangely, and I realized quickly that the last thing a new pastor needs is an offer of friendship coming from someone that he had just met. There were hundreds of people clamoring for Blake's attention and probably the thing he needed first was peace and quiet, but, despite my first awkward attempt to become Blake's friend, over the years we spent a lot of time together, and eventually we became true friends.

Blake was my pastor, but he soon became my boss. The choir director and organist for our church left after many years of service, and I stepped in as the director of music. Suddenly, Blake is my pastor, my boss, and my friend. Isn't life complicated?

I didn't go to Blake because he was my pastor, but talking to the pastor was a good move. Whether you are looking for knowledge or building your influence, look at the existing networks of people you want to reach and identify key people within those networks who can help you to spread the word or help you gain crucial knowledge that you need to take effective action.

In my local community, my only network was my church, and Blake was the key influencer within that network. He was also an important connector. Blake knew people that could help and quickly suggested that I talk to two key businesspeople who were members of the church.

Blake didn't really tell me much about their background. It was a good thing I didn't know exactly how successful they were before I met them. If I had known, I wouldn't have been brave enough to meet them, much less present my disaster of a business plan. You see, Edwin Johnson founded the company that developed the original 401(k) plan, and Michael Wert founded one of the largest direct marketing advertising agencies in the world.

Both had taken their companies public for millions. However, their success wasn't what made Mike and Ed so valuable for me. It was their giving spirit. Mike and Ed were simply wonderful people who were willing to spend precious time meeting with an "over-the-hill" programmer with a job security problem.

Ed Johnson and Michael Wert turned out to be two of the most positive, creative, and supportive people on the earth. Despite being extremely busy and successful businesspeople, they went out of their way to help me create my dream when all signs indicated that I was a disaster case on a doomed mission. Repeatedly they told me that I could do it, if I set goals and put my plans into action. I don't think that I ever heard Ed or Mike talk about being decent, but I wouldn't be writing this book if it weren't for both of these two decent men and their attitudes about life, giving, and business.

It might be extraordinary if they did this only for me, but I wasn't the only person that they were helping. There were dozens, if not hundreds, of other people those two men helped over the years. Eventually, they helped to form a business group at our church to aid the huge number of people that they were already helping on a one-to-one basis.

I can't imagine how they kept up. The new group allowed me to meet a very special collection of people—at all stages in their business development—that shared ideas for a number of years and are friends to this day. It also spawned the ideas for working together to grow our lives that inspire me to this day. The most important thing that Mike and Ed taught me was the impact that a single individual could make by taking simple, little actions that really made a difference.

> "Surround yourself with positive, successful people."
>
> —Ken McArthur

The Best-Laid Plans

Back to today's story. This morning, I was reading and answering e-mail and not getting any closer to my goals. What I should have done was write 10 pages for this book and *then* process my e-mail. Finally, I got through the stack of e-mail and back to thinking about my goal.

Yesterday, I planned to do the following:

- Define my goal for this project.
- Think of a title for a printed book that will be a part of the project.
- Write at least five pages for the book.
- Send out an update to *AffiliateShowcase.com* members and let them know what I am doing.

- Make a list of people who can help me meet my goals.
- Start collecting resource materials for the project.
- Think about ways to pre-sell the book.
- Clear out all of my e-mails.
- Fix dinner.
- Take my wife out to see a Broadway-quality play.

Here's what I actually did:

- Defined my goal for this project.
- Came up with a title for the printed book.
- Wrote 10 pages for the book.
- Sent out an update to *AffiliateShowcase.com* members.
- Cleared out all of my e-mails.
- Talked on the phone to customers, joint venture partners, and family.
- Fixed dinner.
- Took my wife out to see a Broadway-quality play.

If you compare the two lists, you will notice that *I didn't reach all of my goals.*

How did that happen? First, I really enjoy writing this book—so instead of writing five pages, I kept going and wrote 10. That's a good thing, because it means that if I keep up that rate, I can cut the number of days required to write my book in half. Then I talked to customers, friends, and family. That's a good thing, too, because I'm building those relationships that are so crucial to my success.

So overall, not too bad. I definitely surpassed Jack's "Rule of 5," and that means I deserve a pat on the back.

> "Make sure you give yourself a pat on the back when you exceed expectations."
>
> —Ken McArthur

It's not always possible to do everything that you put on your list. Things happen, priorities change, and that's a good thing. The list shouldn't be a rigid task list; it needs to be a flexible guide.

Here's a process for you:

- Set goals.
- Take action.
- Measure results.
- Pat yourself on the back or get your act in order.
- Repeat for success.

I promise, I'm going to get to the impact-generating, money-making, business strategies, and technique parts, but the hard cold fact is that the one big problem that faces 99 percent of my clients is taking action on clear goals:

- If you don't have clear goals and take action, you won't succeed.
- If you don't succeed, I don't reach my goals. That's just not an option for me.

Throwing Away My Readers

Okay. I just told you not to listen to anyone who says you can't do it, so what am I going to do next? I'm going to throw away a bunch of readers. I hate doing this, but I have to do it if I'm going to meet my goals.

I really want you to succeed. What's more, I want to help you for as long as you want to keep trying. Nevertheless, the fact is some people shouldn't focus right now on creating massive impact, and that someone may be you. Think for a minute about whether now is the best time for you to create your maximum impact. Some people shouldn't focus on creating maximum impact even if they can.

Don't worry. I stand by what I said before: If you want to have an impact you can. Your impact isn't about aptitude tests or abilities. It's about setting goals, taking action, measuring results, and *persistence*.

If you don't have aptitudes or abilities, you can get help, but if you don't have persistence then all is lost. People with all kinds of mental and physical handicaps have been successful in creating massive impact, so don't let your limitations stop you.

I Have Plenty of Limitations Myself.

I discovered a few of them when I went back to college after 14 years off. My wife wanted me to study computer programming, but I told her that if I went to all the trouble and expense of going back to school that I wanted to study music.

Notice that there seems to be a pattern here. I always seem to be going against the flow. There were a couple of obvious problems with my choice. I wanted to study choral music and composition, but I sang bass/baritone and didn't even know the notes on the bass clef. Luckily, I had some great professors who stuck with me through some heavy learning curves, because I had to support the wife and kids at the same time that I was going to school.

Picture a 30-year-old man with a wife and two young daughters, barely getting by working in a computer store with only a dream of going back to school. Each week there are mounds of bills to pay and each day I spend my time working hard to get by. There are plenty of bills, and going back to school means more expenses and much less time.

I keep my full-time job and add two part-time jobs to generate extra funds, but I know that I really have to push to get through school as quickly as possible. Burnout is a real possibility. I set my goal of getting through a full four-year program in only two years, but there is a slight problem: The university has rules about how many credit units I can take in a single year.

Luckily, my computer background helps out a little bit, and I discover that, if I sign up for four credits under the maximum number of credits, I can keep adding three-credit classes each day without the computer catching the fact that I am carrying double the maximum number of credits.

It's a compromise. I'd love to be taking a leisurely stroll through my education, but finances and family make it impossible. I'm doing well in school, but nevertheless there are problems, and one of the problem areas is piano. Music is a performance major and many of the courses require countless hours of practice for far too few credits. I have zero piano skills, and in order to complete my degree, I have to prove that I am competent playing a piano. I really want to take all of the piano courses and learn how to play well, because I know that it's an important skill to have. Unfortunately, all of the piano classes meet when I have to work.

There is one way out. If I can take a test and prove that I can play the piano well, I can skip the required classes. Bottom line: I need to pass the piano proficiency test. So I find a teacher to tutor me and teach me exactly the skills needed to pass the test. I study hard and when I think I'm ready, I schedule the test. I play "The Star Spangled Banner" in three keys, play from different clefs, jump through the hoops, get my credit, and squeak by the test. I'm qualified! Great!

It wasn't easy and I didn't see a lot of my family for a while, but in two quick years, I got my B.A., started working for my Master's degree, and went looking for a teaching job. That's when my *almost zero* piano skills came back to haunt me.

Music teaching jobs weren't easy to come by, but finally I landed my first interview in Long Beach, California. It was a long commute, but it was an exciting opportunity for me, and I was thrilled. I also had a couple of advantages. Unlike most recent college graduates, I knew how to act on a job interview, and I sounded polished, professional, and amazingly similar to a wonderful teacher. I breezed through the interview and was feeling great about my prospects of landing the job, when the person who was interviewing me said, "One quick thing. Just play this piece of piano music for me." I froze solid.

Ever had that deer-in-the-headlights look? Everything I might have known about piano instantly blew out of my empty brain. I was stunned, blank, and immobile. I was completely embarrassed, fumbled out a few notes, mumbled an apology, and quickly left. After years of sacrifice, work, and study, there was no way I was going to be able to get that job or seemingly any job working in music.

It hit me hard as I went down several flights of stairs to the lobby of the building and I stood there thinking for a long time. Finally, I took a deep breath and decided to climb back up the stairs. Timidly, I knocked on the department head's door and said, "I know that I just completely blew my interview. I just wanted to see if you have suggestions for how I can do a better job the next time that I interview with someone." The kind man told me not to worry, that he understood my panic. We talked for a few minutes, and I even played a little bit of a piano piece that I knew, just so that he would know I wasn't a complete idiot. He was gracious and made a few other suggestions, and I left.

It didn't look good for a job offer, so I arranged to stay with the part-time teaching job that I'd been working at while I studied. It wasn't much, but at least it was experience, and I knew that I needed experience to get a full-time music job.

Unexpectedly, a week before the school year began, I got a phone call. It was the department head from Long Beach, and he had a job offer for me. Although I didn't know it at the time, the head of the music department had been struggling with young first-time teachers. Freshly minted scholars often felt they knew everything there was to know about teaching and wouldn't take advice. The simple fact that I came back up those stairs to ask him for advice landed the job. Despite a lack of piano skills, my persistence paid off, and it can with you too.

Just one thing:

Creating Massive Impact May Be Picking Up Dog Poop for You.

Remember that I told you about Mark Joyner's two options—sex or picking up dog poop—when he talks about what you really want to be doing. The cold hard fact is creating massive impact may be "picking up dog poop" for you. If you don't feel as thrilled by creating an impact as you do having sex, this may be a sign that you don't want to make the investment.

I can hear you now: "Ken, aren't you being a little extreme here?" Maybe, but here's a little-known truth: Creating impact is an addiction, and, if you aren't getting a high from making a difference, it's going to destroy you. As with most addictions, it may destroy you even if you do love it. The only difference is that if you love what you are doing, you will have a great time on your way to destruction.

So, what are some signs you shouldn't be trying this? Try some of these on for size and see if they fit you:

- I can't stand change.
- I need a steady paycheck.
- I don't really like people.
- I can't seem to take action.
- I hate to learn new things.
- I hate doing sales.
- I hate keeping records.
- I hate the government.
- I can't pay the grocery bill next week.

- The landlord just kicked me out.
- Nobody likes me.
- And so forth.

Don't worry too much if you find a few things in the list that fit you. A couple of them fit me.

I love change and love to learn new things, but I don't like accounting much, and the government drives me a little crazy sometimes. I'd be a lot better businessperson if I loved keeping records and doing sales, but no one is perfect, and you don't have to be perfect to be successful. Thank God for that!

What you do have to realize is that you have to deal with many of the things that are on that list if you want to create massive impact, so decide now whether this is how you want to spend a ton of time and money. Do you want to be doing this even when you would rather be doing something else?

Let's imagine that you have me convinced. Creating massive impact is your mission in life. Your spouse, best friend, parents, kids, enemies, and even your competition think that this is perfect for you. People are offering you thousands of dollars to help you reach your dreams. You have 50,000 people waiting in line to sign up.

You will absolutely keel over dead if you can't create massive impact.

Even if You Are a Perfect Fit, This May Not Be the Perfect Time.

I get people contacting me all the time who are at the end of their rope, clawing for threads to hang on for just one more second so that they can take that big swing at changing the world. Don't do it.

I can hear you thinking, "Ken, I have to do this! I'm out of options, I just got a divorce, I'm going into rehab tomorrow, and I can't pay my rent. I can't take care of my kids, the car is being repossessed tomorrow, I just lost my job, and I don't have any job skills even if someone was stupid enough to give me one! I need a purpose in life!"

Don't do it.

I'm not saying you can't have your dream. You can! But now is not the time to start creating massive impact. Don't spend your last dollar on success books, recordings, Websites, info products, seminars, or promises.

If you are down to your last dollar, spend it on food for the kids and then get some help. Go to your religious group, your government, your friends, or your enemies, and get some help. Then find a job that will pay you something (anything) right now so that you can get yourself out of this mess. Get your head straightened out, your body well, and your mind working again.

Keep your dream. Heal, learn, dream, and grow. Try saving a few pennies, but for your own sake don't start to change the world until you have your personal and financial life in some kind of decent order.

Your life doesn't have to be perfect. No one has a perfect life. Face it. You already have a good idea whether this is the time for you. What I am trying to do is to force you to think about it. You need to think about it, even if this is the last thing you want to think about in the middle of your wonderful dream.

Creating massive impact will add to your pressures, not magically take them away. If you can't cope now, adding more to your plate won't help. Be honest. Changing the world isn't easy.

Still Reading?

I'm impressed! You're still reading after all we've been through together, so now let's get to the fun part! There are many ways to create impact. However, the real question is how *you* want to create massive impact. I've gone through some changes in approach myself and tried a lot of different models along the way, so let me tell you what I did, and maybe you can see yourself fitting in somewhere along the way.

I learn best by example. If someone can tell me how he or she did something, I can usually modify that example to fit my strengths and weaknesses. I hope it will work for you too. Modeling the behaviors of people that are doing the things that you want to do is a powerful way to fulfill your own dreams and turn them into reality.

When I started my business I needed money fast and I couldn't spend anything, so the first thing that I tried to sell was my skills. The Internet was starting to take off and people were hearing that they were going to miss out if they didn't get on the Internet. In fact, brick-and-mortar businesses were terrified that if they didn't get online right now, they would be out of business soon.

I knew how to make Websites, so I started farming myself out. First, I went to an existing client and built a site for him. I even talked him into putting my site on the same server as his for a reduced price. So now I had a Website at no cost. On my Website, I created a simple price list for the services that I was going to offer and waited for the sales to happen.

Okay, so you have 20/20 hindsight, and you know what happened. This time you are right: Nothing happened. It's the beginning of the Internet boom; millions of people think that they will die if they don't have what I'm offering. Even better, not many people know how to create Websites. Perfect timing! High demand, limited supply. Still, nothing happened.

This Would Be a Good Time for a Mentor.

Not being shy about asking for help, I met again with Ed Johnson and Mike Wert. Ed and Mike must know every person on the planet between the two of them. What's more, they share all of those wonderful relationships with any person they can help by introducing them to someone else. That pretty much covers all of us.

Ed took me down to meet his friend at the local hardware store. Mike introduced me to the head of a nursing school, and they didn't stop there. Banks, non-profit organizations, research facilities, hospitals, schools, and the list went on and on, person after person until I was able to make a living "on the Internet."

I know what you are thinking. This isn't the "making a living on the Internet" that most people have in mind when they start dreaming about easy riches. Well, it wasn't my perfect ideal situation, but I was making a living and I couldn't have done it without the Internet. The Internet was my brochure, my demonstration, and my clients' Websites were their final product.

Despite all of the help that Ed and Mike gave me, it wasn't easy. I was living job-to-job, hoping the jobs would keep coming, and Ed and Mike wouldn't run out of friends. I was reinventing the wheel each time I did a job, and I noticed that a lot of my clients wanted the same things.

This is where you can start seeing the value of systems. We do some things repeatedly. When you see repetition, start seeing a system. Systems can save you endless hours, and in many cases systems allow you to do the work once and then leverage the system for years to come. I decided to create a software platform that would make it possible to give many of my clients what they wanted without having to write everything from scratch every time. I needed a system.

I also wanted the tools, software, and connectivity that it took to build larger systems, and that took money. Ed and Mike told me that money is not a problem for a good business; all I needed was a great business plan. Luckily, with the Internet boom in my favor—and, more importantly, Mike and Ed casting aside their finely tuned business judgment for a moment—I managed to talk them into investing in my company.

Get a Rock to Stand On: The 3 Essential Ingredients

To have a real impact, you need three essential ingredients:

1. Ideas
2. Time
3. Money

If you don't have one, use the others to get some.

You don't have to have money to start out with—at least I didn't—but you do have to leverage money if you want to have a serious impact. You can beg, borrow, steal, joint venture, sell your ideas, sell your possessions, or sell products and services or part of your business, but, however you do it, you need money for massive impact.

In a tiny way, even back then I was building my foundation for creating impact. I quickly managed to obtain thousands of dollars in computer equipment, a T-1 line coming into my basement for connectivity, powerful software, and a few customers. Soon, I was developing a powerful system to drive portal sites with community features such as chat and forums, and all was right with the world.

Expect Trouble.

About this time, people start figuring out most of the dotcom business plans aren't worth the paper they are printed on. In fact, people wondered if any business should be on the Internet and started thinking that the whole Internet thing is just a big lie. The bubble burst. Suddenly, customers were harder to come by and projects were on hold.

At the same time, I started noticing that organizations that spent $10,000 to $50,000 on my system, didn't use all the features. In fact, they were using our powerful system as a "brochure" site. Heck, I can do better myself!

No matter what you're doing, expect that things won't always go the way you want them to go. That way, you're not surprised when trouble finds you.

Know Your Limitations.

Part of the problem was that I just don't like sales. I have no problem talking to someone once I have an appointment, but cold calling is not my idea of happy. My dream is to have the people come to me. I will be thrilled to help them when they come in the door.

Deep down, I know myself—just as you know yourself. When I was 20 years old, I'd owned my own pet store and loved it. People would see the sign and walk in the door and I'd be there to help them out. It was perfect. There were no doors to knock on. The question became, "How can I get people to walk into my store on the Internet?"

When I started my company, I had big plans for taking my company public. I was learning that I love working for myself. I also learned from Mike and Ed that taking a company public is similar to having a job. If I tried to take a company public the way my friends Mike and Ed did, I'd be right back to working for someone else, or I'd be out on my ear again.

By this time, I had several sites of my own, but the sales pattern was clear. The sales were all coming from local companies, not from people who wandered into my Website. There were a few exceptions, but face-to-face sales were the rule. So, how do you get many customers to walk in the door? First, you have to find the people.

When people first started dreaming of making a living on the Internet, Jim Daniels was one of the early pioneers. Jim took $300 and started his online business. After just six months, he was able to quit his "real" job. Now, Jim earns much more than he ever did working for someone else, but he didn't start out being an expert on the Web.

In early 1996, Jim used a $300 tax refund to buy a used IBM 386 computer. He hooked the computer up to the Internet, and for several months he researched how to start and market an online business. In his research, Jim found some great materials and soon put together 40 pages of great tips for starting a business online. Those notes became the basis for Jim's first publication, *Internet E-mail! Beyond the Basics!*

Jim did so well selling his manual that he soon realized that he was making more from the Internet than he was with his regular job. In order to stay in touch with his customers, Jim put together a newsletter, the *BizWeb eGazette.* I was lucky enough to be among his first subscribers.

I realized that, if I wanted more customers, I needed to find out where they are, and I knew that Jim had many subscribers who could be my customers, so I sent Jim an e-mail. I told him about the software that I created and suggested that we work together on a project. It didn't happen right away. In fact, it took a couple years of e-mails and building the relationship before we finally decided to work together on our first project together. Jim had built up a list of about 160,000 subscribers. That was a group of people.

More important was the fact that his subscribers trusted Jim to give them quality advice and resources for making a living online. Trust level is key in selling products anywhere, but particularly on the Internet, where there are so many people waiting to take your money. However, there was one even more important thing. Jim is quality. "Quality" is important. Life is too short to deal with people who do not bring the highest standards of quality to their life.

Find Quality People With Groups That Trust Them.

Jim and I sent many e-mails back and forth, but we never talked on the phone. In fact, we still haven't talked on the phone to this day. We never signed a contract or legal agreement, and yet we did more than a quarter-million in sales in the first six months of our project. I'll be sharing much more about how we did it soon.

I hear you thinking again. "But Ken, I'm not some hot-shot programmer; I don't have investors; I'm just an average person trying to get by. I barely have a cent to my name. What does this have to do with me?"

Well, first, there are no average people. People are extraordinary! Ask any human being on the earth to spend a full day telling you the story of his or her life. If you sit there and listen, you will be amazed, guaranteed. Every person brings something unique to the table. So stop worrying about what you think you can't do and concentrate on those five things that you *can* do today.

Start looking at your skill set—you wouldn't be here today if you didn't have any skills—and start thinking about how you can use them. If you can't think of skills, just make an attribute list.

Let's do an example:

- 18 years old
- Female
- Has worked in a gift shop
- Has worked in a camera store
- Has taken photography classes
- Christian
- Has worked for a pony ride
- Was a Girl Scout
- Was in 4-H
- Played flute in the band
- Traveled to England
- Lived in the country
- Lived in California
- Lived in Missouri
- Lived in Pennsylvania
- Likes horror fiction
- Studied ballet
- Took gymnastics
- Has grandparents
- Has parents
- Has siblings
- Knows people who grew up in the Sixties
- Went to a prom
- Got dumped by a boyfriend
- Dumped a boyfriend
- Got lost
- Had a friend on drugs
- Knew someone who died

The list can go on forever, and everything on this list is an experience that you can use to impact another person. Imagine what you can come up with if you have lived more than 18 years!

Start Assessing Your Skills.

Try on some of these skills for size:

- Public speaking
- Writing
- Networking
- Sales
- Video production
- Graphic design
- Programming
- Website development
- General computer skills
- General business skills
- Generating "back of room" sales
- Interviewing others
- Getting targeted traffic to a Website
- Putting on a teleconference
- Leading a discussion group
- Motivating a forum
- Using search engines
- Conducting research
- Getting qualified leads
- Converting leads into buyers
- Creating joint ventures
- Creating podcasts
- Being a radio host
- Hosting a television show
- Writing a newspaper column
- Creating information products

There are many skills that you may have right now. You can quickly develop other skills and, what you don't have now and can't develop, you can always outsource. What you want to do right now is start listing the skills that you do have, so that you can leverage them as you develop new resources and systems of your own.

Start by taking a good long look at how you got to the place you are right now. Your knowledge, skills, and experiences are what have carried you to the successes that you have experienced already. When you first got started, where did your clients come from? Why did they buy from you? How did you attract them? Which skills have they depended on? Which skills have produced the most income for you? What kind of new skills would you like to develop? What activities excite you the most each day? What skill makes you the most proud?

You will find many more revealing questions that will make you really think about all of the wonderful skills that you have right now to leverage your impact when you use your Impact Assessment Tool at *TheImpactFactor.com/resources.* For now, just think about the possibilities, and start listing the skills that you can use to leverage your impact in a notebook.

When I started my business, I had a few skills to work with, just as you do. Some of those skills I used to leverage my impact, and others I ignored. Along the way, I developed new skill sets. Just to give you an idea of the type of things you might want to look at, I'll tell you about a few of the skills and a few of the gaping holes that I had in my skill sets when I first started building my own system.

First, I was lucky enough to have some programming skills. At the beginning of my career, those skills set me apart from thousands of people who were eager to start a business on the Internet, but lacked the basic computer and programming skills that I developed during my programming days.

I had a few people skills. In general, people find me likeable, honest, and dependable. I try to do the things that I tell people that I will do and although I'm not always successful, I try to make things right when I'm not. People skills can take you a long way. If you sincerely enjoy working with other people, then you have a head start when you want to make a difference.

The list of skills that I didn't have was much longer.

I'd never done public speaking, been interviewed, developed an information product, or built a list. I was a lousy salesperson, was terrible at keeping business records, didn't know anything about graphics or video production, or had never even been on camera or done a podcast.

My point is you can do any of these things and you can develop skills quickly. Start making two lists right now. The first list is all the skills that you can leverage right now, and the second list is skills that you want to develop. Those lists will be very helpful when you use the online Impact Assessment Tool to develop your action plan.

Let's start looking at your impact goals. When you start setting goals, try to avoid some of the common mistakes in goal-setting:

- Setting too many goals.
- Not being specific.
- Creating goals that can't be measured.
- Setting goals that aren't relevant.
- Developing goals that aren't realistic.
- Setting goals that have no time limit.
- Not putting goals in writing.
- Setting goals that are too easy.
- Framing goals negatively (for example, I will not eat cake for a month).
- Not understanding why you want to achieve a goal.
- Not setting priorities for your goals.
- Setting goals for things that you can't control.
- Setting goals that you don't want to achieve.

When I first left my "real" job to start my own business, my goals were simple. I wanted to replace the income that I had with my job immediately and gain the freedom of not having a boss.

Sure, I had many other wants. I never wanted to depend on a single customer. I wanted to avoid cold-call selling. There were many possible goals, but keeping things simple helped me to focus on the bottom line. I needed to pay the bills; I wanted my freedom—now.

So there weren't too many goals to focus on. The goals were measurable; I knew exactly how much money I needed to make to replace my current income. There was a time frame even though it didn't sound too realistic. My goals were very relevant, I definitely wanted to achieve them, and it was something that I could control. Even better, by having that pressing focus I was able to replace my income and have my freedom immediately.

To accomplish my goals, I leveraged the skills that I had, identified real problems that my potential customers needed solved right then, and found solutions to their problems. I also identified key influencers within my existing networks and developed real relationships with them so that they could help me spread the word about the solutions that I had created.

The goals that you set today will change as your impact grows. Once I replaced my income and had my own business, I could move on to bigger goals. I want to encourage you to define your purpose and start setting those first goals. The Impact Assessment Tool will help you do exactly that. From there, it's just one simple step at a time to amazing impact.

But the first rule of impact is to remember to...

Solve a Big Problem

Want a million dollars? All you have to do is solve a problem. In fact, if you are a math whiz, you can have your pick of any of seven problems. All you need to do is solve one and the Clay Mathematics Institute will give you one million dollars. Solve all seven problems and they will give you seven million dollars. Here's an example of one of the seven problems from Clay that looks easy. It's called the "P vs. NP Problem."

Imagine that you have a big family. It's been 20 years since the last family reunion, but Aunt Susie, in all her socializing glory, has managed to extract promises from 400 relatives that they will definitely come to a family reunion that is only two weeks away. Unfortunately, there are only 50 rooms available and you can only put two people in a room.

In her ever-convincing way, Aunt Susie has decided you are the most organized person in the family—how she got that idea, I don't have a clue—and she has put you in charge of housing accommodations for the event.

There are a couple of problem cases, though. Some of the relatives don't exactly get along all that well. Luckily, Aunt Susie knows everything about everyone in the family and she has compiled a list of pairs of people who should never—under any circumstances—room together.

On the surface, the problem isn't all that difficult. All you have to do is compile a list of potential roommates and then check it against Aunt Susie's list to make sure that none of the pairs that are on her list have somehow gotten matched together on your room-mates list. It sounds easy, right?

Computer scientists call this an "NP Problem." With a computer, it's very easy to check to see if one of Aunt Susie's "Do NOT Let These People Room Together" pairs appears on your rooming list. All you have to do is put both sets in the computer and ask it to look for matches. With an easy program, today's slowest computer can do that in less than a second.

But, who should get the available rooms? Wouldn't it be nice if you could just input the names of the people who are coming to the reunion and have the computer pick which people get the housing? Just imagine that you write a program where you can enter the names of all the people and Aunt Susie's list of mismatches, and have the computer produce a final list of randomly generated roommates guaranteed not to have a mismatched pair.

Unfortunately, it turns out that it's not that easy. The total number of ways of choosing 100 lucky relatives from the 400 people that want to come is greater than the number of atoms in the known universe.

Even if you had a supercomputer, you would never be able to solve the problem by brute force—checking every possible combination—within your lifetime. However, there is nothing that says that, with a little bit of creative programming you couldn't come up with a way to solve the problem. In fact, I challenge you to do it; after all, it's worth a million dollars.

One of the biggest problems in computer programming today is identifying situations where it's easy to check the answers to a problem, but, even though it's a simple thing to check, it would still take too much time to solve by any computer. The roommate problem seems to be a problem that can't be easily solved by a computer, but no one has proven that it can't be done. In fact, maybe you could do it.

In 1971, Stephen Cook and Leonid Levin formulated the problem as a mathematical equation and asked people to solve the problem as "does P (easy to find) = NP (easy to check)?" Stephen Cook's description of the problem actually runs 12 pages of detailed mathematical specifications, but the basic problem is fairly simple.

If you could solve this problem, the world would be grateful and you could be a million dollars richer. If you don't like this problem, the Clay Mathematics Institute has six more problems you could try.

But, What if You Aren't a Math Whiz?

Luckily, all problems are not math-related, and there are millions of problems just waiting to be solved. That's a good thing, because, if you want to have an impact, you need to solve a problem.

Think about it for a minute. If there's nothing wrong, you can't fix it. If there is nothing wrong, no one will care if you *do* fix it. If no one cares about what you do, no one will notice you, and you will have zero impact. So, if you truly want to have a really big impact, you'd better start with a really big problem.

I know that you are feeling overwhelmed right now. I've been talking about huge problems that don't have an easy solution, and you thought that I was going to make your life simpler. You are right to feel overwhelmed, because, when you set out to solve a big problem, it's overwhelming! Just what you need, right? Another big problem without a solution!

Fortunately, there's an easier way to solve big problems. If you want to solve a big problem, you should start with the little things.

Imagine two sisters who both want to write a best-selling novel.

Cathy is brilliant and educated. She studies with the finest writing teachers at a world-class university and she associates with some of the most well-known authors in the world. She is thinking about her book and constantly comparing her ideas to the great thinkers around her. Each day she writes a little and measures it against her competition, and each day she tosses her work into the wastebasket with a sigh because it doesn't meet her standards.

Tricia has lived in the shadow of her brilliant older sister for all of her life and does not dream that she will ever be as smart or as educated, but she is compelled to write down her simple thoughts each day. At the end of each week, Tricia reviews the thoughts that she has written and looks for the flashes of life that occasionally sparkle in her simple words. Tricia constantly trims and polishes the gems that she finds and saves the scraps of her thinking in her idea bin. Each day she builds and improves and each day adds to her skill.

You know as well as I do who will write the best-selling novel. If you want to solve a big problem, you need to take it one step at a time and break it into manageable pieces.

> "Building your personal legacy takes time. Since you have limited time, you should work on something that matters."
>
> —Ken McArthur

If you were at jvAlert Live in Orlando or Philadelphia or the "Get Your Product Done" workshop in Atlanta, you may have met a dynamic ball of energy that was all smiles and all heart by the name of Muriel Moton. Muriel is easily the most positive and uplifting person in ANY room. Her smile glows, and she is contagious with her enthusiasm and energy.

It's hard to imagine that anything could have ever gone wrong for Muriel, because she sounds as though she's never had a problem in the world. However, if you think that Muriel is so positive because life is easy for Muriel, you are dead wrong.

In 1988, Muriel returned from her honeymoon in California and decided to go through the garage and get things organized. As she was sorting through boxes, she noticed an unfamiliar credit card with her name on it. In fact, as she looked more closely, she found more and more credit cards in her name and a stack of unopened bills from the credit card companies. Muriel was in shock. The credit card statements showed that her new husband had stolen her identity. What happened next wasn't pretty.

The state suspended her driver's license because her husband bought a car in her name and then allowed the insurance to lapse. Muriel's newly minted marriage was in shambles. Finally, the last straw was when Muriel's husband reached out and grabbed her arm and told her, "If you ever leave me, I will kill you. Do you understand me? I will kill you!"

I'll let you read the rest of Muriel's story and how she overcame so many problems in her upcoming "sure-to-be-best-seller" book, *Live Life Like It Matters,* but for now I'll just mention that Muriel overcame those problems and many others that followed and now impacts people constantly, literally all over the globe.

For nearly 10 years, Muriel has shared the principles that are vital to preserving, protecting, and maximizing human value and potential for personal achievement and fulfillment, and organizational development—one person at a time.

Imagine going to Malawi, South Africa, Zimbabwe, and Kenya, and having an amazing impact on people all over the world. Muriel has done that. But it doesn't matter where Muriel is. Muriel has impact on every person that she meets, which is why I mention her in this book.

Bottom-Up, Not Top-Down

Muriel found some powerful ways to solve some very real problems, and then she started to share those solutions with the people around her, the same way you can.

I haven't asked Muriel, but I tend to think that Muriel wasn't thinking about becoming rich or famous when she was sitting on the garage floor crying her heart out. In fact, she was pretty emotionally devastated, just as anyone would be. But, the story isn't over. Muriel has had some pretty amazing impact already, and, with the launch of her book, I'm sure that impact will only grow.

If you want to have impact similar to Muriel's, you need to start from the bottom up, not the top down. Instead of thinking "I want to be rich and famous," try thinking about how you can solve a big problem and share the solution with others. Once you start sharing a great solution, it can never be stopped.

Just as Juan Mann was, Muriel's presence will be felt. But, unlike Juan, Muriel has a plan to make it happen. Muriel is getting some great advice from some pretty amazing people who are thrilled to help her every step of the way. Part of that is because Muriel is constantly enriching their lives with her amazing attitude and open heart. Who wouldn't want to help that kind of person? I know that I do.

As we build your personal impact system over the coming months, I want to help you increase your impact in some very specific ways, but first you need to know that, if you really want to have a big impact, you need to solve a big problem. Solve that problem and people will be thrilled to spread your impact all over the world.

First Look for the Pain, and Then Look for the Solution.

The good news is that the world is full of problems waiting to be solved. You have a wide choice of problems to select from. According to my friend

Christine Comaford-Lynch, people all around you are hurting and all you need to do is look for the pain. Listen when people tell you something hurts.

Christine has quite a history. Bill Gates refers to her as "super-high bandwidth" (I guess he should know, because he dated her.), and former President Bill Clinton, in a letter to her, thanked Christine for "fostering American entrepreneurship." *Newsweek* says she's "the person you want to partner with."

Christine ran away from home at 16 to become a model in New York City, became a Buddhist monk, broke her vows, decided to become a millionaire, made $10 million dollars, gave away $3 million to non-profits, retired at 40, and got married to the man of her dreams. Sounds great, right? She also blew it a lot. Now that's something you don't hear about much!

Christine lives a very interesting life, and she shares much of it in her new book, *Rules for Renegades.* She recounts her first date with Bill Gates, who she met when she was a contractor for Microsoft, and pokes a little fun at his methods in the romance department. She also talks about dating Oracle's Larry Ellison, and encounters with Barbara Walters and the Clintons. Christine learns something useful from them all.

As a five-time CEO/entrepreneur, she has defined new markets, developed products to serve them, and executed sales, marketing, and product strategies. Throughout Christine's 20-year career in business, she has started five of her own companies, all of which have been acquired or taken public, assisted 700 of the Fortune 1000, and advised to the White House. But it wasn't always like that.

In 1989, Christine was a temporary contract programmer working for Microsoft when, after years of using independent contractors in place of employees, Microsoft began feeling some pain from the IRS. Under the IRS guidelines, the independent contractors were actually employees. Picture this: The IRS wants Microsoft to pay withholding taxes. Now they've come down hard, and Microsoft needs to either convert them to actual employees or make sure that they are working for other companies—quickly.

Christine is attending a meeting for all of the independent contractors with the "Dark Overlord of HR." The independent contractors love being independent. They are taking home great paychecks and loving their freedom, and suddenly they are told that they must either become employees or be hired by a new job shop, Volt Technical Services.

Christine is scanning the room and doing the mental math. There are 300 contractors in the room. With an average margin of $10 per hour going to Volt, no wonder those guys are smiling so big. How hard can doing payroll be? In a shot, Christine raises her hand and says, "I have a company. I'll employ everyone. Plus, my firm takes a smaller cut of the employee's paycheck than Volt."

The first problem is that Christine doesn't have a company—at least not yet. Luckily, Christine remembers that if you have a hundred dollars you can form a Delaware corporation in ten minutes. The second problem is that she knows nothing about processing payroll. Christine gives her dad a quick call, and he suggests that she outsource the payroll processing, and by evening she has 35 new employees.

Microsoft was in a world of hurt because of the IRS crackdown. Christine was able to provide a solution to ease that pain quickly. Now Christine looks for the pain constantly—even while standing in line for coffee.

Fast forward to 1995. Christine is standing in line for coffee at the local Starbucks. The guy standing in line with her is talking about the pain of marketing consumer products on the Internet. He doesn't understand the technical issues, but Christine certainly does. Over the next few months they decide to launch a company to deliver personally targeted coupons and promotions directly to consumers. Within four years, Christine sells her shares for a few million.

I have a real passion for helping entrepreneurs build sustainable businesses, and I've worked with a lot of people who wanted to start a business on the Internet. The Internet is an amazing vehicle for generating high-profit offerings with minimal investment, but thousands of people try to start an Internet business without solving a real problem. In fact, most people are asking the question, "How can I make money?"—when they should be asking the question, "How can I help?"

Yesterday afternoon I sat down with a group of top-level marketers to brainstorm the question, "How can someone with $100 to invest build a business that grosses a million dollars a year in a short period of time?" Interestingly enough, there are lots of ways to do it, but when all of the ideas were out there on the table, someone thought to ask the question, "Why?"

Why would you want a million dollars in the first place? Believe me, I'm not against the idea of you making a million dollars a year, but if you just stack it up in the corner and count it over and over, it's not going to make a difference in your life or anyone else's. Bottom line: It's not about having money—or it shouldn't be—because having money doesn't *do* anything, and, if you want to have an impact, you have to do something.

> "Impact doesn't come from 'having.'
> Impact comes from 'doing.'"
>
> —Ken McArthur

Jeffrey is short and eager. If you close your eyes as he talks to you, you can almost imagine a puppy. For most of his life, Jeffrey has been a plumber, but now he has caught the Internet marketing work-at-home bug. The lifestyle sounds very attractive to Jeffrey. He's done his homework and listened to lots of Internet marketing experts. He's played around with some of the ways to make money on the Internet, but now he is ready to get serious.

Jeffrey's wife is getting a little concerned. She wants to support Jeffrey, but she's worried about the finances. So far all of the cash flow has been going out of the family budget and she hasn't seen a cent come back in. Jeffrey says that it's an investment in his education, and he's right, because you can't make real progress if you don't educate yourself. On the other hand, there comes a time when all the education in the world won't help you make a dollar. As my friend Sterling Valentine says, "If knowledge were power, librarians would rule the world." Studying how to take action doesn't get you results. You need to do something.

Jeffrey is just steps away from making a big mistake. It's a mistake new businesspeople make all the time. In fact, experienced marketers make the mistake repeatedly and they are still able to make money in many cases. It turns out that making money isn't all that difficult on the Internet. Jeffrey can just put together a simple e-book, create a Website, and let people know about it, and with a decent sales letter Jeffrey can make some sales. A number of my friends have made sizable incomes from doing just that.

It's so easy to sell products that many times we get caught up in the ways to wring more money out of marketing tricks and forget why people are buying the product in the first place. People are buying products and services or looking for ideas to fix problems—not to be conned by marketing ploys.

Imagine Jeffrey's choices. The world is wide open. He can develop products and services about anything, but the first thing that comes to mind is that he loves Internet marketing. He's new at it, but he eats up every bit of information that comes into his e-mail, so Jeffrey decides to take that information and make his own e-book about making money on the Internet.

Jeffrey's choice is not unusual. People do it all the time. A quick Google search returns more than 55,500 results for the specific phrase *Internet Marketing eBooks*. There are thousands of free ones available. Where Jeffrey is headed, literally hundreds of thousands of people have gone before. The "How to Make Money Online" problem has been solved repeatedly in different ways since the beginning of the Internet.

My friend Rosalind Gardner has made a healthy living by selling a simple e-book that she wrote years ago, but a closer look will show that it's because she solves a very real problem for people and she gives some very real direction. People can get information easily. What they need is something that solves their problems.

Think of it from your own perspective. You are reading this book because you want to have more impact, not because you want more information. If you follow this proven system, you will get more impact—not more information about impact. That's why I want you to create your own systems to solve problems.

Think of how much more valuable Jeffrey's product would be if, instead of delivering more and more information about making money online, he actually gave his customers a system that would do it. I'll have a lot more to say about building your own systems in Chapter 12, and you will definitely want to be wide awake when you read that chapter, because your personal impact system is crucial to make your impact grow and allow you to live the life that you want to live.

But, even if you have a system and it solves a real problem, it won't make any difference if you don't ask one simple question.

Give Them What They Want

*T*ime magazine says that Craig Newmark is one of the 100 most influential people in the world, but you might not notice him if you passed him on the street. If a friend gives you Craig's phone number and tells you to call "Craig" for some business advice, Craig would answer his own phone and listen to your problems and give you some good, solid, common-sense advice. In fact, he still does some customer service, so he gives advice to many people who don't have a clue that they are talking with one of the most influential people in the world.

Having a conversation with Craig is similar to talking with a good friend. The first time that I talked to him on the phone, the conversation felt like any other one that I might have during the week with one of my friends who has a site on the Internet. At the end of the call you are thinking, "What a nice guy! Of course I knew all of that stuff, but he really seemed great." You would be right about one thing: Craig Newmark really is a great person.

> "Listening is the most crucial part of any conversation."
>
> —Ken McArthur

In early 1995, Craig noticed people on the Internet helping each other out. He decided to help a little, too, by telling people about events in the local area around San Francisco.

CHAPTER 4

At first, Craig's news about local events spread entirely by word-of-mouth. People in the area talked about the events, and they talked about his list. More and more people got interested in what was going on.

Eventually Craig's List grew large enough that they needed to get a "list server" called majordomo, to get the word out to a growing "list" of people. At some point in the setup procedure, majordomo required a "name." Craig wanted to call it "sf-events," but his friends convinced him that "craigslist" was a more personal and down-to-earth name, so he named one of the most visible sites on the Internet after himself.

Once Craig got the "list server" set up, the system e-mailed event information to members of the list, and members of the list could contribute event information to the group. Eventually people started posting information about other types of things. They posted jobs, things they wanted to sell, and rental apartments, and Craig's List grew. Craig wrote some software to add e-mail postings automatically to a Website, and *www.craigslist.org* was born.

In 1997, advertisers approached Craig and asked him to run banner advertising on his site. At the time, banner advertising was the "hot" way to make money on the Internet, but Craig decided to take a non-commercial approach. According to the official Craig's List history (*www.craigslist.org/about/mission.and.history.html*) Craig said at the time, "Some things should be about money, some shouldn't, and I make enough doing contract programming." Remember that this was in the middle of the dotcom orgy of greed. There was a reaction to that greed that started a real community, which in turn started a "community" movement to run local face-to-face parties to make the sense of virtual community more "physical," and Craig's List grew.

Finally in 1999, Craig went full-time. Now more than 15 million people use Craig's List every month to post more than 12 million classified ads, and there are more than 50 million postings in more than 100 forums. So how did Craig's List go from 12 subscribers to 15 million people a month? Craig and I talked about several key factors. The first factor that came up in our conversation was luck.

> "If you want to go off like a lightbulb, it helps if you are standing in the right place at the right time, and lightning strikes."
>
> —Ken McArthur

Craig started his list at the start of the boom times in the Internet, in a community (San Francisco) where many influential people were connected and very excited about the new technology. However, there were thousands of classified sites on the Internet—some of them probably run by very nice and very bright people, and most of them don't even exist anymore.

Part of the reason that Craig's List is so big is that it's been around for a long time. What Craig had to do was survive long enough. Remember: Today is the start of your next project. If you are waiting beyond today, you are losing the early-mover advantage.

> "Starting early at ANY time is the perfect time to start."
>
> —Ken McArthur

Starting early was an advantage, but starting early is not enough. Craig and I talked for quite a while about all the factors, including timing, simple approach, the technical challenges, user interface, customer support, community growth, the use of media, controversy, community, and key people, but, if I really wanted to, I could boil everything that Craig had to say into a few key factors.

Craig Newmark's Bottom Line

1. **Craig created something that people already wanted.**

   After looking at what people were asking for, Craig gave it to them in a way that was simple and useful.

2. **Craig listened to customers to find out what other things they wanted.**

   Customer service is not a back seat item for Craig Newmark. He actively listens to what people ask for and then makes a decision about whether he can provide that solution or not.

3. **Craig followed through and actually did something about what his customers wanted.**

   Many people say that they are going to help you with your problems, but most people don't ever get around to doing it. Action beats inaction almost every time—and it makes you stand out in a noisy world.

Do you think Craig's answers are a little basic? It might be tempting to think so, but personally I don't think Craig's answers are basic at all. I think Craig's answers are the core to his success. If Craig hadn't been listening and solving his customer's problems over the long haul, his site would have faded with the thousands of other "also-rans."

Find out what people want, and then do something about it. Maximize "word-of-mouth" and the "kindness of the press" by treating people the way you want to be treated and giving the best service that you can. Simple is what we all need, so use the simplest tools possible. That's a simple tool for your success, too.

Craig Newmark, the creator of Craig's List, still works in the customer service department, and there's a reason why he does it. When we listen, we can solve the problems that the world wants solved and the world will scream for our solutions.

Watching Your Backside

L et's talk about money for a minute. I'm about to tell you the story of someone who was struggling to get started. He had a great mind and some good skills—just as you do—but despite trying time and time again, he just couldn't seem to get a successful project done.

He didn't like the feeling. Who wants to feel that you have tons of potential, so much to offer, and then nothing happens? You are struggling to make ends meet and the world seems to be an endless loop, going nowhere. That's a tough way to feel, and it's not uncommon. How many times have you started projects and never finished them? How did you feel?

How would you feel with some real success? My new friend's feelings sure changed shortly after we met. With a little help from many people, he was able to have some incredible success and generate a sizable amount of income in a very short period. The money he earned didn't solve everything, but it did make a difference. That was a very good thing.

I know you may be thinking that money isn't the goal for you. If you are, I understand, because money has never been my main purpose in life either. Some people use money as a scorecard to see if their life has a value, but deep down we all know having money isn't the goal. Just having money doesn't solve any problems. Money is a tool, and you need to use it wisely.

Having money can actually create problems. If you think that money problems all go away because you have a million dollars, you are unfortunately mistaken. I've known some unhappy millionaires.

Even so, any way you look at it, money is a key leverage point for creating impact. Think money doesn't make a difference? Try doing a search on Google for *closed for lack of funding.*

Closed for Lack of Funding

The University of Minnesota's AIDS Clinical Trials Unit was one of the first federally funded AIDS research sites in the country. More than 2,000 volunteers have enrolled in the studies to receive treatment as they help researchers learn about the safety and dosage levels of new medications while they explore the many facets of HIV/AIDS research. Now it is very likely they may be forced to close due to lack of support.

The University clinic's closing is a setback for the entire Midwest, because people with HIV/AIDS will no longer have access to cutting-edge research and treatment. Those 2,000 people won't be helped. Many times that number won't benefit from the research that might have been done at the center. That's a big impact.

But the clinic is just one story. The stories go on—literally millions of listings of programs that have lost their funding are struggling to keep operating or almost gone for good. But, it's not just huge public institutions or non-profit organizations that need funding. If you intend to make a lasting impact, you need to make sure that your personal financial foundation is secure.

Creating products and services that increase your impact while you generate funding to support your goals is crucial to long-term success. This is true for any organization and for you personally. Now that you have a solution to a real problem, I want to help you maximize your impact with products and services to compliment and support your long-term goals.

It's Getting Easier Every Day.

Luckily, creating products and services that increase your impact is getting easier every day. Over the past 10 years, there has been exponential growth in the availability of tools to create more and more professional products. People who would never have thought that they could create their own products and services are creating these products every day. That means that you have many options.

Just look at the publishing industry and you will know what I'm talking about. Printing a book used to be a huge deal. Not so long ago, you used to have to type your manuscript on a typewriter or write it by hand. Then someone had to typeset it. Now, you can type it into a word processor, import it into a PDF file, and send it off to a print-on-demand publisher who can print copies one at a time.

Look at the ways that graphics tools such as Photoshop have enabled non-artists to create professional-looking graphics. Inexpensive cameras have made it possible for you to shoot high-definition video in your house, and digital audio recorders give sound quality that wasn't even imagined 10 years ago.

The Power of Information Products

One of the easiest and fastest ways to create almost instant income for any organization or individual is to create info products. In addition to providing streams of income to help you meet your goals, they also help to spread your message, so you are killing two birds with one stone. This is especially true when you leverage the power of the Internet.

What makes info products the darlings of Internet marketing? Quite simply, info products have been responsible for more Internet marketing success stories than any other product or income strategy. Here are a few reasons why:

- When people need information, they head for the Internet, and they will gladly trade money for information if you can solve their problems or satisfy their needs.

- You can develop information products quickly. In many cases, you can have a product ready to sell in less than a few days. Traditional offline publishers typically take six months to a year to release a book. This means you can have a number of products ready in a very short time, and you can beat the big boys to market.

- Your information products can target small, but profitable niches virtually ignored by the big corporate publishers.

- They can often be created (or found) at a cost of zero dollars, but produce an income that many doctors and lawyers would envy.

- No warehousing or shipping department is required, especially for downloadable information products. But I'll show you how to avoid the warehousing and shipping hassles, even if your product has a physical component (DVDs, CDs, and workbooks).

- The right information product can establish you as an expert in your niche, opening the door to more products and profits. Wouldn't you like to be the 800-pound gorilla of your niche?

- When you launch an information product properly, you create additional opportunities for income by attracting joint venture partners who will want you to sell their products, too. Many marketers earn more money selling other people's products than they do selling their own.

- Multi-million-dollar companies have been founded by a single information product. Maybe yours can be next.

You can build your info product income in many different ways. You can sell a single product for $5,000. You can sell hundreds, even thousands of smaller products such as $27 e-books. You can also sell a broad mix of different products at different price points. Build the revenue stream that meets your needs and your pace. You can see the obvious appeal of information products: low margins, high profits.

Information products are nothing new. Before the Internet, people made millions selling information products. Boardroom and Nightingale-Conant built their empires with course packages of books, audiotapes, and videotapes. The Internet merely made it easier and lowered the cost of entry. That's where the problem is. Anyone can create an information product. Just look at ClickBank and the thousands of information products for sale there. Many of the folks selling products on ClickBank barely make enough money to cover their Website hosting costs.

Now, there's absolutely nothing wrong with those people. Most are smart, hardworking and energetic. After all, they actually went out and took some action, right? The problem for those people who never seem to get ahead is in the "how." Many people learn just enough to take action. In fact, they're told that taking action is a good thing, that those who take action are the winners. That's correct—mostly, but consider this.

Suppose you enter a long-distance marathon, such as the Boston Marathon. You're lined up with thousands of other runners, waiting for the starting gun to go off. And when that shot rings out, you turn around and run in the opposite direction—away from the finish line instead of toward it. You've taken action, but are you likely to win, or even finish, the race? Of course not.

But that's exactly what happens when you create and sell an information product without a plan. You're running away from your goal, away from the money, and away from everything that money can bring.

Getting the Edge

With proper planning and support, you'll create an information product that goes to work for you. It becomes part of a system designed to pull money toward you in ever-increasing amounts. That's when you'll earn money even while you're on vacation or sleeping, and that's the secret the world-class Internet marketers know. Now it's your turn to get the same edge they have.

From Nothing to $100,000-Plus in 92 Days

That's what happened to Sterling Valentine. When Sterling started out, he had no product, no joint venture partners, no large list, but he quickly became an impressive success and has gone on to create some amazing impact. So let's explore how that happened.

I first met Sterling at the very first jvAlert Live event. I'll tell you a little more about that event and how it got started later, but for now I'll just let you know that jvAlert Live events are a place where some of the top Internet marketers in the world get together to create some pretty amazing multi-million-dollar joint ventures.

When I met Sterling, he wasn't a millionaire. In fact, he was still struggling to find the kind of success that most marketers reach for, but always seem to fall short of achieving. Have you ever had a great idea, started on an amazing project, and then—well, somehow it just doesn't happen.

Let's just say Sterling had a bunch of unfinished projects on his plate. Sterling's parents taught him, if you wanted to get something done, you needed to do it yourself. That clear vision found a home in his brilliant brain, and he believed it, until the day that he realized the fact that no one can carry a grand piano up a flight of stairs by himself. Somehow, that image stuck in Sterling's mind and made him realize that we exist to help each other.

Sterling had already had a close-up view of his mortality after finding himself with a gun to his head in a Philadelphia parking lot, wondering if his next breath would be his last. His eyes were closed and he felt a calm come over himself, even in the moment as he waited for fate to touch his life. When he at last opened his eyes and found the gunman gone, he was grateful. Tattooed on his forearm is the word *fortunate*, and he feels fortunate.

Standing Out in the Crowd

At the jvAlert Live event, Sterling stood out. When new people come to a jvAlert Live event they tend to hurry around from one high-powered marketer to another trying to convince them to become involved in their latest project. Their first thought is, "What can this person do for me?" Sterling was the exact opposite. As he talked to every person at the event— whether it was a powerful top-level marketer or someone just starting out— Sterling's question was always, "What can I do to help you?"

By the end of the event, everyone knew Sterling. The most influential people wanted to talk to Sterling and all of the people at the event would have been thrilled to support anything that Sterling wanted to do. That's the power of looking out for others first.

As the event came to a close, Sterling and I were sitting together on a couch in the lobby of the hotel along with my good friend Frank Sousa. (We later became the famous "Three Guys on a Couch" because of what happened, but I'll tell you about that later.)

Sterling and I talked until the wee hours of the morning. We both knew that we couldn't get where we wanted entirely by ourselves. Sterling explained how he finally realized that he needed help, and he wanted me to mentor him on his project. He shared his goals with me, his ideas, his dreams. His timing couldn't have been better. I explained to him how I was planning a product of my own. My product would teach anyone—even a total newbie starting from scratch with no product, no joint venture partners, and next to no list—how to develop a viable (and profitable) info product and bring it to market successfully. That product was *Info Product Blueprint.*

Keep in mind that I've worked with many of the biggest names in Internet marketing for years. They're on my speed dial, and they accept my calls. I've advised marketers at every level, brokered deals, and been directly responsible for helping people earn millions of dollars of income on the Internet.

I can honestly say that I've had my fingers in nearly every aspect of Internet marketing. Yet, in all my years, I had never deliberately set out to mentor someone from start to finish. I wanted to prove I could transfer my marketing knowledge and experience to a newbie, and take him or her from 0 to 60 in record time.

Ready to Take Action

Now here was Sterling—ready, willing, and able to take massive action—but lacking the guidance and structure that someone with my years of experience could provide. Meanwhile, I needed a relative newbie who would put my plan to work, someone willing to become my "proof of concept" test pilot. I needed a "marketing guinea pig" to prove that my theories about creating successful information products and taking them to financial success would actually work in the real world.

Sterling made a challenge to me that night: If I would mentor him, then he would help me by documenting his progress on video from beginning to end, and beyond. The fact that, until now, no one had completely documented this sort of project only made it more appealing. The video documentary would became the core of *Info Product Blueprint* and stand as proof that I could deliver as a mentor and teacher. It would remove the mystery of what it takes to succeed in Internet marketing. And it would prove to any beginner that success is possible if you have the right coach to guide you.

The timing worked perfectly for both of us. Our goals were in harmony, and a new joint venture was born.

I'm not recommending that you create your information products the way Sterling created his first information product. Sterling was "one of a kind"—just as you are—which means that what worked for Sterling might not work exactly the same way for you. All that said, you can certainly learn from his experiences, which is exactly why I wanted to videotape the experience every step of the way. It is a huge value when you can watch someone go through a process first and model his or her successful process yourself. That's all a part of building your own successful system and it makes your success much more likely to happen. Watching Sterling go through the process was an amazing inspiration and learning experience.

Part of the key to Sterling's unique situation was that he just hadn't been able to get a product finished. He had started many projects, but finishing them was a definite challenge. To make things even more difficult, Sterling's doctors said that he had Attention Deficit Disorder, and that meant problems staying on tasks long enough to complete them.

Money That Makes a Difference

After we completed our project, Sterling was able to use some of the money that he earned from the project to consult with a leading brain specialist, who discovered—after years of frustration caused by misdiagnosis and inappropriate medication—that Sterling had considerable physical brain damage caused by childhood injuries. Bottom line: Even though Sterling was literally a genius, he was fighting the fact that large portions of his brain weren't working at all.

Part of the wonderful impact that Sterling received from completing his project—and by generating some much-needed income—was that Sterling was at last able to get the medical help that he needed to function at his personal best. Who says money doesn't matter?

A Date With Drew Barrymore

As we started our project, those dreams were in the distant future. The real problem was selecting a project and getting the work done. Sterling was starting out with nothing. He had no significant customer list, no product, no joint venture partners, and just a few ideas to start with. Until one night my wife brought home a DVD from the local video rental store called *My Date with Drew*.

Here's the story behind the movie. Brian Herzlinger has been crazy about Drew Barrymore since he was in the second grade. He first saw her in *E.T.* Nothing too strange there, but now it's 20 years later and he's decided to try to fulfill his lifelong dream by asking her for a date. Only one small problem: She's Drew Barrymore, and he's a broke, 27-year-old aspiring filmmaker from New Jersey.

Brian and his film school pals decide to do everything they can think of to convince Barrymore to go out with him—and document their quest along the way. Unfortunately, they are short on funds. He doesn't even own a video camera to make the documentary. Luckily, it turns out, you don't need any money to buy a video camera these days, thanks to Circuit City's 30-day return policy.

What Brian does have is $1,100 that he won on a game show—where the winning answer was, unbelievably, Drew Barrymore. Brian uses his winnings to finance the project and buys a video camera, counting on the fact that he can return the camera to Circuit City in 30 days and get his money back. That means he and his friends only have one month to accomplish their mission.

Working on the theory of six-degrees of separation, Brian and his friends set off to negotiate their way through an army of publicists, agents, producers, and assistants who surround the star, so Brian can get to Drew and ask her out.

> "If you don't take risks, you'll have a wasted soul."
>
> —Drew Barrymore

At first look, the movie—and Brian—seemed a little strange. I wasn't totally convinced that I was going to love it, but what the heck. I like Drew Barrymore myself, so it can't be all that bad. Twenty minutes into the movie I'm cheering Brian on in his quest and knowing that this is going to all end badly. Sure enough, Brian reaches the end of his 30 days and suddenly the video goes to still photographs of Brian taking the camera back to Circuit City, still without meeting Drew. It's a heart-touching moment, but, in the famous words of Internet marketing, "But wait! There's more!"

It turns out that the Internet comes into play in more than one way. Brian decides to put up a Website of his quest and he posts a video trailer of the movie that he wants to make. Even though his 30 days has past, he is persistent and starts to get a little publicity for his Website. Then one day he lucks out and gets interviewed on a drive-time Los Angeles station about his quest for a date with Drew Barrymore. Website traffic jumps up, and the word gets back to Drew Barrymore's production company. I'll let you watch the movie to see whether or not Brian gets his date.

So what does this have to do with Sterling? Think about it for a second. Sterling has no extra funds, no great resources. Sterling needs a deadline, because public accountability is one of the most powerful motivators that exist. Imagine Sterling announces a very public challenge to create a product, find joint venture partners, launch a product, and make $100,000 dollars in only 90 days. Then imagine that we document it each step of the way á la *My Date with Drew*.

The first thing we needed to do was to decide on a topic. After some brainstorming, we decided one of the important factors in reaching success for his project was creating some powerful joint ventures. Why not learn about joint ventures from some of the top marketing experts in the country while we created the product and developed joint venture partners?

Learning From Napoleon Hill

Sterling started by using a journey similar to one taken by Napoleon Hill for his classic 1937 book, *Think and Grow Rich.*

> "My goal was twofold: Extract 'the secrets' of success from the greatest Internet marketing minds of our time and create an in-depth course that would allow all who view it to quickly attain similar success themselves."
>
> —Sterling Valentine

In an exhausting quest to achieve his goal, Sterling was lucky enough to get face time with the most distinguished names in online marketing, and he did it by asking the simple question, "How can my product help you to achieve your goals?"

I'll tell you more about Sterling's quest to create his first information product later, but for now just know that, just as Brian Herzlinger didn't, Sterling didn't meet his deadline either. But, Sterling wasn't too disappointed. He managed to complete his product, line up joint venture partners, launch it, and complete $101,153 worth of sales in a total of 92 days. That's not too shabby.

Creating the Blueprint

But that's just part of the story. We completed a six-DVD set of videos that documented the entire process and packaged it into a huge package called *Info Product Blueprint.*

Sterling describes *Info Product Blueprint* as a "complete Internet marketing encyclopedia." Others who have previewed the package call it "an Internet Marketing University in a box." Maybe "university" is closer to the truth, because if you pop the flaps on the hefty carton, you'll meet a faculty of 45 marketing "professors," representing a full range of skills, experience, and specialties. If it's related to information products, you'll find it in *Info Product Blueprint.*

One of my critical requirements was to make it comprehensive, but manageable. I needed to cover the entire info product process, but make it simple and easy to follow.

When I say the entire process, I mean everything. That included all phases of creating and preparing the product for market—from market research, product creation, and copywriting, to outsourcing and fulfillment. Then there was the launch-building side—scheduling and tracking all phases of the launch, while generating buzz and attracting JV partners and affiliates. At the same time, we continue to work on your business, putting in the foundation that will take you beyond your first info product and into a real, long-term, high-income business.

Despite the sheer volume of information I wanted to include, I knew I had to keep it practical and accessible. That's why I set out to create a program flexible enough to accommodate different learning styles and levels of expertise. In order to do that I used a combination of video, audio, an easy-to-use workbook, and complete transcriptions to let people pick the method of learning that works best for them.

In your own information products, I'd really encourage you to embrace a large variety of learning styles. That way people can pick and choose the materials that work best for them and still get great value out of what you are offering.

Comprehensive is good as long as you don't scare people off. Be sure to let them know that if they've already put most of the pieces together, but need to fill in a few crucial gaps that are keeping you from reaching your goals, then take only what they need.

Want help finding the right niche with plenty of hungry prospects? You can get that help quickly and easily. What about the right way to build a list of proven buyers, the kind who will enthusiastically stuff your bank account to overflowing? You'll find out how in minutes.

My team of experts and I organized *Info Product Blueprint* to deliver exactly what you need when you need it. When you design your own products, make sure that you are addressing your customers' desires for crucial information when they need it.

I've been around since the "Dark Ages" of Internet marketing, and I'll admit that I know the lay of the land pretty well. I'm sure that, given enough time—and there's never enough of that—I could have put together a respectable course on information product marketing.

But "respectable" wasn't what I had in mind. I wanted to create the "definitive" info product course. This course would be the one that every marketer would keep within arm's reach of his or her computer. To create such a course, I needed to draw on the best and brightest minds. I picked up the phone and started calling in favors. I wasn't taking no for an answer.

Building a Dream Team

By the time I was finished, I had assembled my dream team. Notice that I didn't build this product by myself. I'll have much more to say on building a team soon, but for now know that you don't have to do it all yourself, and, in fact, you shouldn't!

I know how tough it can be to get started. I've been there myself and I've watched hundreds go through every phase. They invest time, sweat, and sleepless nights—all the time wrestling with the uncertainty of "Is it really worth it?" It's truly heartbreaking to watch someone go through this. But it's even worse to see him or her give up. Especially for someone like me who knows how good life can be for those who "make it."

That's why I finally decided to create *Info Product Blueprint.* I saw how desperately new people needed guidance. I decided this had to be the most complete information product, impact-building package anyone ever created. This package had to provide everything you could possibly need to create and launch a winning info product.

If you're interested in more of the story of Info Product Blueprint, you can find out more at *InfoProductBlueprint.com.*

Start thinking right now about what product and service offerings you can add to your personal impact system. You can't keep your message moving at maximum speed if you can't pay the bills.

Note: 1-Shot Wonders

Sterling earns his nice jolt of quick cash and it's great. Now what happens? Suddenly reality starts to set in: $100,000 is not going to last forever. That's not the end of the world. You can always start over and do it all again. I've been there myself. In my early days, each Website that I designed, I designed from scratch. If I wanted more money, I had to build another site.

Luckily, you have options. Because I've been in that trap before, I think I can help you avoid it. I'll be telling you more about how to start building systems and move to recurring, passive income streams as quickly as possible. Remember that your time to create impact is limited, so let me give you a tool that will make sure that your messages spread like wildfire.

CHAPTER 6

Zingwhacker Ideas: Structure Your Ideas to Move Like Wildfire

I magine an unstoppable force concentrating all of its energy on a single razor-sharp point. In an exploding burst of energy, it flashes across your vision in a blaze of white-hot light as it drives a single core idea deep into your long-term memory cells, and then, with a blast of searing heat, welds it to your most passionate emotion forever.

You know this single idea will change your life forever. The idea is so clear, simple, and full of insight that you instantly recall everything good about your own life and you find yourself running to share this amazing new idea with the one person in the world who you love the most.

As you breathlessly approach the person you love, you wonder if you can explain such insight, power, and emotion. You repeat the simple words and watch as your feelings move across the face of the one you love. It was easy.

Simple, memorable, and repeatable ideas hammered into our brain forever with one bold stroke are "zingwhacker" ideas. Zingwhacker ideas have some crucial elements. To make it simpler, all zingwhacker ideas are:

Simple
Intense
Memorable
Pictures
Leveraged
Emotional
Repeatable

The human mind can only retain a limited number of messages in a block. We need to break information into units that can be "bookmarked" in the massive storage dump of information floating around in our heads.

The Young and Old of It

In the summers when I was young, I went to the library nearly every day and checked out a stack of books and read them. What was more amazing was the fact that I actually remembered much of what I read. I went through school barely studying and almost totally without taking notes, and was able to recall the facts that I needed to get through the tests. I didn't have a photographic memory, but my recall was excellent.

Then I started to get older. Suddenly, the memory didn't seem to do as well. I struggled to recall people's names—even if I could recite their entire life story—and I was concerned. Maybe I was developing early signs of Alzheimer's. Fortunately, I knew a geriatric psychologist, so I asked her about memory problems. After all, that was her field of expertise, and if I needed help, I might as well get it early before the whole brain went.

After assuring me that I wasn't in any immediate danger of early Alzheimer's, she was kind enough to explain to me a little bit about how memory recall works. It turns out that I wasn't so remarkable in my youth after all.

Think of your brain as a computer hard drive for a second. When you are born, it's pretty much a formatted, blank disk. There are a few key important bits of data on the disk, so that it knows how to operate, but other than that it's pretty much empty space.

As you live, you collect data. You learn how to get your food. You learn the effects that crying has on your mother, and you store data away. You have a huge hard drive. People have about 100 billion nerve cells and many more cells in the brain that support the nerve cells, so there is room to store lots of stuff.

As a teenager, you've stored at least 13 years of data, but retrieval is quick. Imagine that your brain has its own search system. You put in keywords, and the brain goes out and finds related information. As a teenager, maybe you've known a few hundred people in your life, so if you are trying to remember a name it goes quickly.

Now imagine that you are working on your old computer 40 years later. The hard drive is crammed with information that you haven't used for years. You pull out your trusty search engine and start trying to search for a name and the hard drive grinds and grinds as it searches through countless data looking for that one item that you want to know about right now.

If it makes you feel better, difficulty in recalling things is a symptom of knowing too much—I know I like that point of view! However, that doesn't help us recall things. What helps you recall things is when you create a bookmark in your brain so that you can find it more quickly. You can easily retrieve key information when you bookmark it.

When programmers want to search through a database of information, they create "indexes" so that they can find the information more quickly. Key information is stored in a separate list along with a record number so the computer can quickly locate the information that you want to retrieve. In fact, you can create multiple indexes on the same data. The more "indexes" that you create the more chances you have of finding the data quickly.

If your ideas contain all of the key zingwhacker elements, they will be automatically bookmarked in the brains of everyone who hears your idea. That means that they can quickly and easily retrieve the idea, and repeat your idea to anyone. Plus, they will want to share your ideas, because zingwhacker ideas are tied to the key emotions and memories that we value the most.

Create Your Own Language

Let's start with the word *zingwhacker* itself. Before today, the word *zingwhacker* never existed. In fact, I did a Web search to make sure that there were no listings for that term whatsoever. *Dictionary.com* tells me that there are "no results found for zingwhacker," and I just did a domain name search and *zingwhacker.com* is available to be registered.

By the time you read this book, there will probably be many search results for the term *zingwhacker* and certainly the domain name will be taken, and the term will start a life of its own. In fact, I encourage you to spread the word about zingwhacker ideas. It's clear that more people should know about them, so post an article on your blog, put it in your newsletter, and mention zingwhacker ideas in your books, interviews, and speeches. Shout it on the radio and get it on the news. Zingwhacker is here to stay.

In effect, today I have started to create a new language that is unique to my message and you should do the same for your message. Language is the way that we spread ideas and the words that we use matter. How do some of these words make you feel?

Adeptness	Exciting	Polished
Aptitude	Expertise	Potential
Authoritative	Facility	Potentiality
Bent	Faculty	Power
Brave	Function	Powerful
Capability	Gift	Professional
Capacity	Giving	Proficiency
Comfort	Honesty	Qualification
Command	Helpful	Remarkable
Competence	Impacting	Resourcefulness
Competent	Influence	Self-Expression
Comprehension	Influential	Skill
Controlling	Inspirational	Strength
Courageous	Inspiring	Talent
Dexterity	Integrity	Thrilling
Discovery	Intelligence	Turn
Dynamism	Intimate	Understanding
Effectiveness	Knack	Unlimited
Efficacy	Know-How	Virtue
Empowered	Might	Warm
Endowment		Wise

Words can move people easily and head them in the direction that you want them to move. Let's take a closer look at some of the key elements that make zingwhacker ideas so powerful.

Simple

Mike Rawlings, former president of Pizza Hut, once said, "People are busy, and they appreciate the effort you make. By simplifying, you honor those people."

I know, it's dangerous, but let's take a look at the world of politics for a second. Politicians come in all sizes, shapes, moral persuasions and ethical backgrounds, but the one thing that they do have in common is a need to communicate to masses of people.

Typically, communication comes via some kind of mass media and politicians are talking to lots of people so it can be tricky. After all, not all people agree and some people are downright emotional about what they believe to be true. What's more, the public holds a politician's job in their hands. If the public wants you gone, you will be out on your ear eventually.

To make sure that they are putting their best foot forward, politicians hire media consultants. These consultants teach politicians how to look and sound good on camera, and how to respond to the press and get their ideas across. After all, in politics, it's not what you said or thought you said, but what people heard or thought they heard you say. That means that your words are important.

Consultants teach politicians to respond using "sound bites." To create a sound bite you keep your response very short—10 to 20 seconds—and try to capture the key point that you want to make. By design, sound bites are the *appetizer*, not the *main course*. Sound bites are a clear product of the fact that there is a noisy world out there and politicians need to cut through that noise with a clear, simple idea. Here are a few key strategies for speaking in sound bites:

- Know your audience.
- Be aware of any hidden agendas.
- Know what questions people are likely to ask.
- Rehearse your response.
- Say less, and you have less chance of making a big mistake.
- Make a single point.
- Support your key point with a simple example.
- Restate your point.

You should do the same as you create and deliver your zingwhacker ideas. The brain can only hold onto a maximum of about three ideas at a time, so don't push the limits. "One idea per zingwhacker" is the rule.

This holds true at the micro level and the macro level. Does it mean that you can't express more than one idea? No. But you do need to know that keeping it simple allows you to stick more ideas in someone's overloaded brain. You just need to stick them in one at a time. You can make incredibly complicated systems simple if you convey ideas one at a time. Just imagine trying to explain everything that affects the entire United States. That's what we ask our politicians to do every day.

Think back for a moment to the U.S. presidential race between George Bush and John Kerry. Whatever you think about the merits of the men and their policies, there was a distinct difference in the level of simplicity that they offered to the public.

Bush based everything that he said and did on simple, clear messages. Listen to his speeches, and you can tell that he delivered the same speech almost every time. He only delivered three key ideas: cut taxes, fight terrorism, and control Iraq. Every sentence he used was short and clear. His campaign strategy was just as simple. All he wanted to do was win two key states: Florida and Iowa. Through simple, clear, repeated messages, the people trusted him.

John Kerry had dozens of messages. What he didn't have was simplicity. Bush shut up after his key points, and Kerry kept going until people couldn't remember what he was saying. Bush simplified; Kerry amplified and confused. Clearly, the simpler choice is not always the better answer, but the simpler message always gets through.

But even beyond simple, your zingwhacker ideas need to be stripped down to their core. Not only were the ideas that Bush kept repeating simple, but they were core to the hearts and concerns of the American people. Without Florida and Iowa, Bush could not win, so they were core to his success. As you fine-tune your zingwhacker ideas, make sure that each message is core to your mission. You can't waste bandwidth on ideas that are not mission-critical.

Intense

Don't create half-hearted ideas. If you are going to put your core message out there, you need to buy into it all the way. You can use intensity to grab attention and to make your ideas resonate.

We pay attention to almost anything that is intense or carried to an extreme. Think about the ways that we select colors. Color specialists tell us that red is associated with danger, fire, blood, war, power, energy, and strength. As colors go, red is an intense emotional color.

A doctor could tell you that red speeds up your metabolism, raises your blood pressure, and speeds up your breathing. Red is very noticeable, which is why it is used for stop signs and other warnings. Red may bring on a sexual response, which is why you may think of sex when you think red lipstick. Just the word *red* in print can bring on an intense response. What do you think made Seth Godin's idea of a "Purple Cow" stick in so many minds?

Some people use a very edgy style of writing. In Internet marketing, the Rich Jerk, a well-known Internet marketer, builds a whole persona around being a jerk. It gets lots of attention and people remember it even it they don't like the approach. Just remember that having people notice and remember you may not be your only objectives.

Be passionate about your ideas and make your ideas passionate. Intensity burns ideas into our mind because it concentrates everything in a very small space. Take your ideas to the extreme, and people will remark about them.

Memorable

If you want an idea to spread like wildfire, people have to remember it long enough to pass it on. Soon, I'll tell you exactly how memory works and how you can move your ideas quickly into your audience's long-term memory, but for now just realize that if you want to make your ideas stick, you need to make sure that they remember it.

For now, here's one of the ways that you can help them remember. All you need to do is give your idea a unique name. Names make it much easier for people to remember ideas. That's one of the reasons that I gave zingwhacker ideas a special name.

You can combine ideas to create some great names. I'll be talking about names in much more detail. So for now, just notice that *zing* and *whacker* are words that I combined to create this new name. Each part of the new name gives you a feeling already. Combined they have even more power. In fact, you might call it a mental picture.

Pictures

What comes to mind when you think of "zing"? I'm pretty sure you can't see a zing sitting on a table—or if you can, you have a better imagination than I do. You do have a picture in your mind though. If someone says the phrase "leaping for joy" you probably don't see the letters L-E-A-P-I-N-G-F-O-R-J-O-Y in your head. What you see is a picture of someone jumping high with a smile on his or her face.

Our brain takes letters and words, and transforms them into pictures. Just imagine if you had to read this book one letter at a time. Imagine what a chore that would be! Instead of reading letters, we translate collections of letters into patterns that we see on the page. Then we turn those patterns into sounds and pictures in our mind.

If you want to make your zingwhacker ideas really fly, you need to help your audience move into a clear, vivid picture as quickly as you can. Let's say I talk about vitality, animation, and zest. Then I excite your interest and enthusiasm about smashing ideas into your audiences head with a smart, resounding blow. Does that conjure up any pictures for you? No? What if I talk about 16-pound hammers or cattle prods? Now zingwhacker is more than a made-up word; it's a picture in your head.

Even better, you created the picture. Did you ever read a fantasy book and then see a movie based on the book? Somehow, the movie that the producer creates never matches up to the world that you've built in your own head. People are wonderful at creating their own pictures. All you need to do is plant the key thoughts and lead your audience into creating a better picture for your zingwhacker ideas than you could ever imagine.

Linkage

Systematic External Linkage is the superglue that locks zingwhacker ideas into the brains and hearts of your audience.

Let's start with a simple idea such as "keep kids safe." The idea is simple and it's fairly clear—although it really doesn't say much about what we want our kids safe from. We can systematically start linking this one simple idea to many things that are external to the core idea. Each link will create a stronger bond and weld this idea tightly into your thoughts, feelings, and emotions.

We have senses of sight, touch, taste, smell, and hearing. We can link our idea to any of those senses. Within the sense of sight, we could associate our idea with the color red to create an interruption, a particular picture to convey innocence, or a lightning bolt to make you feel a troubling storm was coming on. We could link a bitter taste to a feeling of defeat or a sweet ice cream cone to happy days. You can connect the touch of a warm blanket to feelings of safety, the smell of freshly baked bread to family, or the sound of screeching tires to danger.

If you systematically touch on every sense, the bond between your idea and your audience will grow. We can do the same thing with emotions or stories, or past associations with trusted people. We can link ideas to divergent fields of studies. Validation of key ideas outside of your own niche will strengthen the authority of your ideas.

All you have to do is to look for external connections. The more specific ways that you can offer ties and validation from external places the better off you are. You can link to different:

- Age groups
- Geographic locations
- Races
- Experience levels
- Religious backgrounds
- Fields of expertise
- Political persuasions
- Types of businesses
- Income levels
- Emotional types
- Educational levels
- Cultural backgrounds
- Media types
- Learning methods

Of course, the list is as long as our list of differences.

Emotional

Our emotions shape our actions. We remember things that grab our emotions. We buy emotionally, we talk emotionally, and we spread ideas emotionally. If your idea isn't tied to emotions, then it won't reach its maximum impact. People rationalize their decisions based on facts, but they make their decisions because of the way they feel.

In its advertising, the Olive Garden uses a tag line: "When you're here, you're family," which is a purely emotional idea. They don't try to tell you that their lasagna is better, that their bread is fresher, or even that it costs less. What they are selling is your memories of what it means to eat a great meal with your family.

Advertisers often use fear and humor to motivate their audience. However, you need to be careful when you start using these elements. If you use fear as a motivation, you better be providing a solution and, if you use humor, you better make sure that your message isn't being lost. Humor is an attention-getter, but how often have you laughed your head off at a commercial only to wonder what they were selling after you watched it?

Repeatable

People can't spread your message if they can't say it easily and comfortably. Does your idea roll off the tongue easily? If you ask someone to repeat your idea can they do it? Try repeating your idea several times in a row, or tell a child your idea and see if he or she can spout it right back at you.

Get Started Now

Take a few ideas and start using this SIMPLER system to create your own zingwhacker ideas.

Turn the page, and I'll show you some ways to start getting your zingwhacker ideas noticed.

Nail the Quality, Build the Buzz

Tricky tactics and perpetual publicity won't keep your message spreading if you don't have the quality to back it up. Noisy or controversial publicity techniques may get you noticed in the short term, but quality always wins.

The problem with marketing is that it all feels the same. We are indifferent to most advertising because it looks and sounds similar, and we don't really find any compelling reason to believe it. In fact, our minds are so overwhelmed by constant information that we can't process it all. Visual images, sounds, smells, and ideas all come pouring in from every direction. In order to make sense of the world, our brain deliberately focuses our attention on just a few things and blocks out the rest.

In order for your audience to hear your message, they need to be aware of you. I want you to cut through the mass of information and force the audience to focus on you and your message. What allows you to cut through the clutter is the irresistible combined force of the thoughts, experiences, and associations that you create for your audience. If you don't create that massive impact in the mind of your audience, you will never be noticed.

I want you to move from background noise into the full conscious and focused attention of your audience. Once you have that attention, you need to move quickly into their long-term memory, because it is very rare to be able to maintain focused attention for very long.

Endel Tulving performed experiments in the 1970s to prove that there are two different types of memory. Episodic memory—as the name would imply—stores episodes from a person's life. The other type of memory that Tulving was looking at is called semantic memory. Semantic memory stores knowledge—concepts and facts.

Tulving says that the two types of memory are different physically, but there are some types of memory that don't fall neatly into either category. In addition to concepts, facts, and our experiences, we often need to remember procedures for performing tasks. Procedural memory is what lets us remember skills and acquire habits.

Finally, we have a special type of memory that is "unconscious." Implicit memories exist, but they can't be retrieved. Even though we can't retrieve those memories consciously, they may affect our behavior. We talk about implicit memory in cases of amnesia or in early childhood memories that fade. They are there somewhere, but we just can't get to them.

That makes four different types of memory: procedural, semantic, episodic, and implicit.

What we want to be able to do is to move awareness of our message from the semantic memory—short-term memory that disappears when we go to sleep—and store it in procedural memory, because procedural memory is long-term and helps people remember exactly what you want them to do. That's a good thing if you want someone to actually do something.

Memory Tricks

Here's a memory trick that is a 2,500-year-old process that allows you to memorize lists of words of as many as 100 items. If you spend about 30 minutes memorizing certain pictures, you will be able to remember at least 25 words forward, backward, or in any order.

All you have to do is visualize 25 picture-words in your mind. They can be anything, but here's an example for the first three:

1. Picture a single blade of grass rising out of a sea of sand.

2. Picture two yellow eyes glowing in the dark.

3. Picture a triangle because it has three sides.

You get the idea. Now continue until you have 25 pictures in your head.

Next make a list of 25 random words. Then combine each word with the picture that you memorized for that position. Let's say that the first three words are *baby*, *cake*, and *golf*. All you need to do is picture a baby playing with that single blade of grass, a cake with two glowing yellow eyes for frosting, and a three-sided golf course. With a little practice, you will be able to have someone call out any number and recall that picture to retrieve the word that you associate with it.

Notice that what you are doing is actually linking different sections of your brain to enable you to retrieve information more quickly and accurately. If you want to make things even easier to remember, then you can create more links. Try linking visual images with smells or introducing emotions. You can even link whole stories to an object.

If a picture is humorous, painful, or emotional, you will be able to remember it more easily.

If we can use memory tricks to remember things—it's probably obvious to you—we can use the same tricks to help our audience notice and remember our messages. When you create a message, you want to create a strong image that immediately engages your audience. Emotion can also trigger associations that make your message memorable.

Ghost Stories

I still remember the first time I ever went to a story-telling event. There were a number of wonderful story-tellers, but the last performer was a master. You could feel it in the air as her enormous body filled not only the chair, but also seemingly the entire stage. She was strikingly black, but her clothes breathed fire in blazes of yellow and red that seemed ready to burst into flames at the slightest touch. Her fingernails extended at least six inches beyond the tips of her fingers, arching in curves and dotted with glittering stones.

Her voice was deep and resonant as she arched her back, straightening up with a fearful stare, and quietly she began her ghost story. Every sound of the room, every creak of the stairs, every breath was audible as I hung on each word, down to the final scream.

The next day (after a somewhat restless night) I gathered my two daughters and told them the amazing story—word for word for 30 minutes. Every single tone, every motion, and every sound burned into my memory, and I could picture her sitting on the chair telling her story for months afterwards. Still 20-plus years later, I remember that moment and see the image.

Why? Think for a moment about the things that stuck in my head from that single half hour so many years ago. It wasn't just the words. The sound, the sight, the emotions, and the story brought those words to my mind and burned them in my long-term memory.

So what do you need to get your message to your audience and burn it into their long-term memory? You need all of those linkages. It's the emotion, the sight, the smell, the taste, and, most importantly, it's the story.

Everyone has a story. What is truly unique about you and your story?

Herbert Sings the Old Stuff.

Herbert Khaury was born on April 12, 1932. He grew up in the Washington Heights area of Manhattan. His father was Lebanese, his mother was Jewish, and he didn't make it through high school. What he did have was an intense passion for American popular music written starting in 1890 through to the 1930s.

He wanted to be a singer, so he learned to play the guitar and ukulele. In the early 1950s he performed under a stage name of Larry Love and was featured at a lesbian cabaret called Page 3 in Greenwich Village. At first, his parents tried to discourage him.

In the early 1960s, he decided to take the name of a character in a story and started to build a cult following. Eventually he appeared in the film *You Are What You Eat*, which gave him enough notice to get a booking on a popular comedy series, Rowan and Martin's *Laugh-In*. No one had seen anything like him.

Soon he was a frequent guest on the *Tonight Show* and appeared on the *Ed Sullivan Show*. He was eccentric to say the least, and his personality was more of a draw than his music. In fact, he was obsessed with bodily cleanliness and had a distinct distaste for sex that his Catholic upbringing might have influenced. He was attracted to women, but thought that it was sinful to give into those feelings. At one point, he hired a person to help keep him from giving in to his own lust for his attractive female fans.

His first album sold more than 200,000 copies. He got married, but they lived separately most of the time. Their marriage only lasted eight years. Herbert continued to perform around the country and made some good money, but he wasn't very savvy with business and people often took advantage of him. By the early 1970s, Herbert's popularity was fading. He performed any time, in any place where he could find a spot.

In 1984, he married a 23-year-old woman, but they didn't live together much. Herbert joined a circus for 36 weeks. After 10 years the second marriage was over. In 1995, he married for a third time, and in 1996, while singing his most famous song, he had a heart attack on stage and died an hour later.

> "Out, out, brief candle! Life's but a walking shadow, a poor player that struts and frets his hour upon the stage and then is heard no more: it is a tale told by an idiot, full of sound and fury, signifying nothing."
>
> —William Shakespeare,
> *Macbeth* (Act V, Scene V)

That might be my entire sad story about Tiny Tim, except for the fact that everyone has a story to tell.

I owned a recording studio in the late '70s in Tampa, Florida, and I had a regular customer who would come in from time to time to record his songs. He was just a kid, really, who would come into the studio with his girlfriend. They both followed the music scene intensely and seemed to be typical "groupie" types to me. They told me tall tales of hanging out with the Beatles during their recording sessions, and I didn't believe a word of it.

One day he came into the studio, whisking me off to a corner so that we could talk without anyone hearing us. Tiny Tim was in town and wanted to come by the studio, but no one could know, he said. Thinking I'd believe it when I saw it, I went back to work, but before long my young friend came back and sneaked in the door. He made sure that no one except for me was around before bringing his friend Tiny Tim in the door with his trademark ukulele.

I'd like to say that I was a Tiny Tim fan, but I wasn't. I had pretty much the same impression of Tiny Tim that most people had in the late '70s: He was a mental mess, the brunt of more jokes than one person can possibly imagine bearing, and down on his luck playing in dives. I hated to see him that way, but I definitely wasn't a fan. To me he seemed sad and more than a little ridiculous.

Herbert Khaury walked in and sat on a stool. I set up the recording, he began to sing, and the stories came out.

The amazing thing was that he didn't say a word to me. The story was in every song that he loved. You see, Herbert loved that music from a long-gone era with a passion that went beyond words. He knew every song, every artist, every recording made in that amazing historic period of music. He lived the emotions, felt the drama, and probably smelled the cities that the songs lived in. It was a long-gone age, but Herbert was living it that very moment.

I hated to admit it, but I was awestruck. I sat there for two hours while Herbert Khaury lived in the music and poured out his soul. It was three people in a small recording studio, recording a tape that never played again. That was the real story of Tiny Tim—or maybe it was Herbert Khaury—hidden inside of the shell of a person waiting to come out.

You Have a Story.

Everyone I know has a story. It's waiting to come out and be shared. It would be so much better if you could get your real story out.

You have a story, so what are the key elements that you need to get it out? That's where memory kicks into the picture again. It won't do you any good to tell your story if people don't remember it, and it won't do you any good if they hear your story and it doesn't make them take any action. Every message that you deliver should have a clear call to take action. You need to tell the buyer exactly what you want him or her to do, whether you do it implicitly or explicitly.

Get your audience's attention by creating a strong picture in their mind. Keep your messages in action by using action words. Ask good questions and prove your points. Good messages are music. They have a zing and flow to them. Give them touches that polish, refine, and sparkle. Your audience should feel their emotions, but keep things simple. Make one point and lead them to one clear action.

Don't leave your audience's impression of you up to your audience. Who knows what they might decide! You need to tell them exactly what to think about you.

Have You Ever Served on a Jury?

When you walk into a jury room for the first time, people immediately start sizing each other up. Almost immediately, a few individuals start to stand out. Some of them may be very vocal, some appear to be quietly intelligent, and others seem silly or rude. Within the first 15 minutes it is probably apparent who will be the jury foreperson, and from that point on you are a long way toward a final verdict.

We all know the opinions of the group as a whole modify the opinions of individuals within the group. If a person feels that the majority of the jury is leaning towards a guilty verdict, the person will be less likely to voice an opinion that indicates that the defendant might be innocent.

If what the group thinks is going to influence you, you have to figure out what the group really thinks. One way to figure that out is to listen to comments that the individuals in the group make. It's logical to think that if most people are expressing thoughts that imply that the defendant is guilty, that it must be the group's opinion. What makes us think that? It's the repetition of the statements by multiple people that convinces you that the group is thinking the same way.

Apparently, it doesn't even matter whether the repetition comes from multiple people or a single person. Jury consultants tell their clients repeating a consistent theme is an effective way to influence the jury. Jury consultants call the practice "anchoring," and it's a way to convince the jury that the group thinks a certain way by repeatedly expressing the opinion that it's so.

The same thing holds true for focus groups. What we believe other people think influences our opinions, and we get our opinion of what they believe through simple repetition.

If you want people to believe and spread your message, you need to have a clear, simple message that people can remember and repeat. To get them to believe it, you need to repeat that message consistently every time you can. If you want the media to tell your story for you, then you need to define exactly who you are and what your message is. Then all you have to do is get them to keep repeating it for you, and people will believe that it is true.

Relating to the Public

Everyone can increase their personal impact by using what we now call public relations (PR, for short). Edward Louis Bernays is one of the founding fathers of the profession of public relations, but many of the techniques have existed for as long as humans have had to communicate with more than one person at a time.

Bernays combined crowd psychology with the ideas of his uncle, Sigmund Freud, and tried to influence the opinions of the public. Bernays believed that the public was irrational and dangerous because it acted as a "herd," and so he believed that informed people needed to control the herd by influencing the public's actions.

Today when most people think of public relations, they think of press releases, but actually the field covers much more than that. Some of the areas public relations may cover include product placement, publicity, product launches, management of reputations, management of issues, investor relations, labor relations, and crisis management. In fact, public relations covers just about any action you may take to influence what the public is thinking. If you want to affect masses of people, then you definitely need to make sure that you are handling public relations correctly.

You can develop many skills to get your message heard. If you haven't used the Impact Assessment Tool to help you figure out your next steps, you should start there. The tool will help you define your goals and match them to the next steps you need to take right now to get your buzz in motion and start you on your want to unbelievable results.

Getting a Little Bit Famous

We are going to talk about how you can get some buzz started for your idea, product, or service, but first we need to talk about making you at least a little famous. Depending on your personality, this will make you very excited, make you a little nervous, or throw you into a complete panic.

Either way, I need you to consider this carefully. Ideas spread from person to person. We relate stories to people. We relate products to people. People are what make the world go round, and so you have to be involved personally. You may not be comfortable with that fact.

There are several reasons why people may not want to become "famous." Face it: Real fame is a big hassle. Would you really like to be Britney Spears? Fame has its perks, but real fame is an intrusion on your life. Believe me: You don't want to have the fame of Tiny Tim either. If you think that people say nasty things about you behind your back, just imagine being him.

There are degrees of fame, and you get to choose your degree. Maybe you would simply like respect. Maybe you want to be well-known, or maybe you love fame and would love to have a cast of thousands pounding at your door. Whatever you want, you first need to picture yourself in that role.

Imagine That You Can Do It.

Before I could become a speaker, I needed to imagine myself speaking. Today, I still do that before every speech. If I don't take the time to imagine myself giving the entire speech, I can't present it in a way that is comfortable and believable.

Before I could be a book author, I needed to imagine myself writing a book. Whatever you want to do, you can't be it in real life, until you believe it in your head. Don't worry: You don't have to be entirely convinced from the moment that you start.

When I started creating the videos for *Info Product Blueprint,* it was difficult for me to imagine sitting in front of a camera and being on a DVD. Sterling Valentine sat me down in front of a huge backdrop, under the white hot lights, and wired me for sound, and I was pretty much frozen, both brain and mouth.

The first few times I was nervous, and it showed. I still remember starting more than a half dozen times because I couldn't seem to get the first sentence out, and I imagined at the time that I would never be able to get through the entire session. Then Sterling told me there would be no more retakes. One shot, straight through for 30 minutes, and that was it. Do the best you can, good luck, and here we go! Finally, I was able to talk, because I had no choice.

Become the Expert.

One reason people don't decide to be famous is because they don't consider themselves experts. Everyone is an expert in something! When I was in graduate school, I discovered exactly how long it took to become an expert. Some authorities say that it takes about 10 years or 10,000 hours to become an expert. Luckily, most of the readers of this book are more than 10 years old. But, what I discovered was that you are an expert if you know more about something than the person that you are teaching.

My professor was brilliant, talented, and very well educated, but I quickly discovered that I could very quickly know more than my professor knew about many subjects. All that I needed to do was narrowly define the subject. I was studying music and had a special interest in requiem masses. My professor knew a lot about requiems from his broad education, but within a day or two I could learn more about any particular requiem than he ever wanted to know. Suddenly, I was the expert and my professor was a potential student, as long as we kept the subject to the Faure Requiem.

You can do exactly the same thing in any narrowly defined niche. Thank God that you don't have to know everything, because no one can.

The next reason that people don't become famous is pure fear. What would happen if you completely bombed? I know how scary it can be to think about the idea of being interviewed on radio or television, seeing your picture plastered all over the Internet, or hearing the sound of your recorded voice. Maybe you are 20 pounds overweight, look like a dog, and sound like a chicken. Can you be a media personality? Can you count the ways?

Look the Part.

Imagine the amazing variety of body types, looks, and voices that you see on television today. If you can't find someone who is uglier, heavier, and worse sounding than you are, then you aren't looking hard enough. As media consultant Mike Koenigs says, "Get over it!" The easiest way to do that is to concentrate on the reasons that you are doing this in the first place. If you are thinking of what you are doing to help other people then you won't be as focused on yourself. That means that you will be more relaxed and natural, and that people will see your giving heart and love what you stand for. It doesn't get better than that.

There are lots of reasons that you want to be an expert. Finally, people will be coming to you, which means that the days of cold-calling potential customers may be over for you. Even if you are calling people who you don't know, they will be aware of you and what you stand for, which makes it a lot easier to get your foot in the door and for people to feel as if they know you.

Just the fact that you are perceived as an expert pre-sells all of your ideas, products, and services. And it certainly extends your advertising budget. Your expertise is something that can give you unlimited publicity and "free advertising" so that you can gain credibility and generate sales without even thinking about it.

The more people see you as an expert, the more you can charge for your time, your products, and your services. People will recommend you to their friends just because you are an expert, and being an expert removes competition by making you and what you are doing unique in the marketplace.

Meet the Media.

Here's the good news: There are more media outlets than ever, and they need what you can give them. Do you think the media is doing you a favor by telling your story? The truth is that they need you. All that you need to do is take consistent action to get your stories out on a regular basis.

Do you remember Jack Canfield's plan to do at least five things each day? Well, Jack also had a plan to do at least one media interview every day. Big or small didn't really matter. What Jack was looking for was consistent action. If you keep taking action day after day, you will get results.

Each type of media has strengths and weaknesses. Some types of media are trusted more than other types. People tend to believe that television news is credible, whereas they consider news put out by Internet bloggers inconsistent in reliability. Print media targets specific niches better than broadcast media. Radio targets more narrowly than television. Attention spans vary from media to media, and the methods of generating responses varies, too.

The Internet is a relatively new type of media, but it's rapidly moving into wider acceptance. If you are looking for headline news, the Internet is hard to beat. You can also reach highly targeted markets, and the information available on the Internet can stay available for many years to come. It does have its downsides, though. Attention spans are very short on the Internet, and it is one of the least reliable forms of media when it comes to accuracy.

What you want to do is to blanket all of the various forms of media. Remember that, just as people have different learning styles, they are also attracted to different types of media. People who are visual learners may prefer to watch television; auditory learners may be attracted to radio. People who like to read will be attracted to print media at the same time that people who want detailed specifics may choose to research their interests on the Internet. These audiences may overlap, but, if you don't reach out to all of them, you are leaving people on the sidelines and will never generate your maximum impact.

Do Your Homework.

Remember that all of the forms of media are really looking for an audience, just as you are. If you can create content that attracts that audience for them, then you are valuable to that media. The media is looking for news. That means you need to concentrate on new content—no old tired rehashes of information that has been around forever. Controversy also sparks interest. If you are trying to publicize ideas, products, or services that have been around for a while, try to put a new spin on things. Look at what is new in your niche, and you can find new news to tie to ideas that have been around forever.

Urgency is also crucial. Make sure that you let people know that they need to take action now. That includes the media. Try tying your promotions into specific dates or holidays to make sure that the media doesn't decide to wait on your story. Remember that the media get releases all the time, so make yours easy and timely. Be sure to enclose everything that they need to run with the story immediately. You certainly don't want them waiting on you.

Research the publications that you want to publish your story. Watch or listen to the shows, know who the hosts are, read the articles, learn the key personalities, and find out what they are saying. Try to figure out what is important to the key people that decide whether to run your story. Help them reach their goals.

Don't worry too much about whether you are starting big or small. Usually it's best to start with smaller outlets to get practice before moving onto the larger media outlets, but that's not always the case. Your topic may be racing across the news, and you may be in demand from day one. If that's the case, just dive right in and learn from the experience.

The key steps to generating publicity are:

1. Identifying your goals.
2. Finding your target audiences.
3. Locating the media that cover those audiences.
4. Creating and clarifying the story that you want to tell.
5. Specifying the action that you want your audience to take.
6. Getting your message to the media.
7. Following up to land the spot.
8. Performing as a champ when you have the chance.
9. Leveraging what you've done in as many ways as possible.

Getting people to notice you is just part of the battle. Do you remember that naked cowboy in Times Square? He got noticed, but he didn't get his message out. To get your message out, you need to know the secrets of how good ideas travel, and you need to know the secret fuel that keeps them moving.

Person to Person: How Good Ideas Travel

Great ideas, products, and movements spread person-to-person, one step at a time, so you have to make sure you motivate people to get the word out about your ideas, products, and services. What makes people tell other people about our ideas? It's all spelled out here.

Don't Make These Mistakes.

Let's look at a few things that might keep your ideas from being spread. It's much easier to find the mistakes that other people make, so let your imagination run wild as you try to identify some classic mistakes that other people make when they want their ideas to move quickly.

Imagine that your best friend, Sue, shows you a brand new mystification, misdirection, and obfuscation device called a portmanteau unobtanium handwavium. You are very impressed so you immediately run to the telephone to tell your mother. What's the problem?

Luckily, Sue is a very prolific thinker and not easily discouraged by your lack of success getting the word out about the portmanteau unobtanium handwavium. Sue eagerly tells you that she has figured out a way for anyone to watch movies without paying a cent. All they need to do is qualify for the Academy of Motion Picture Arts and Sciences, and wait until the studios send out complimentary DVDs at Academy Awards time. She asks you to get the word out quickly about this new discovery before someone discovers the loophole and the opportunity disappears. Can you help?

No? Sue puts her thinking cap back on and quickly returns, waves a finger in front of your face, and tells you that you will never have a cold again. As it turns out, she appears to be right. The next day you do not have a cold. In fact, as time passes you wait for a cold to appear, but you seem to be in perfect health. In the meantime, Sue has left the neighborhood and you have no clue how she performed this feat. Can you spread the news about this miracle?

Sue devises a system for eliminating human solid waste by partitioning it evenly among her 10 closest neighbors. Because of the nitrogen value, Sue assumes that her neighbors will be thrilled to accept her offer of a valuable resource. Can you make this system universal for Sue? Just let people know about the great value that they are getting.

Sue decides to give real value to her audience, so she agrees to give $1 to every person on the earth if you will donate matching funds. Are you interested in spreading the word?

Due to her diligent work, Sue discovers the Fountain of Youth, unfortunately, there is a curse on the fountain, and anyone who tells where it is dies within hours. Shall we call the national news networks?

Finally, after testing ideas for years, Sue cures hunger with a simple easy, low-cost pill. No one who takes it will ever require food again. There are no side effects. Tests show that people can live indefinitely just by taking a single pill. The only person that Sue trusts to tell the world is you, and no one believes you.

What do you think? Sue could keep trying for years, but somehow she just can't seem to get the word out. The answers seem obvious to you, but it's not quite so obvious from where Sue is sitting.

It turns out there are some key elements that you need to spread any idea, product, or service. People spread news, so, if you want the word to spread quickly, think about how people operate and why they do the things that they do.

Is it easy to talk about a portmanteau unobtanium handwavium? Sesquipedalian obscurantism may be fun for a bit, but if you want to move an idea quickly, you need to make sure that people can actually talk about your idea. If people can't use their own words to discuss your ideas, they won't talk about them at all.

What Makes an Idea Easy to Spread?

Here are a few properties that make an idea more likely to travel quickly:

- Simple to say.
- Easy ways to get the word out.
- Rewards you if you spread the news.
- Valuable.
- Automatically spreads by making more.
- Benefits everyone who gets it.

Spread Your Idea to 30 Million People.

Let's take a look at an idea that spread to 30 million people in less than 30 months and see if you can spot some of the properties that made the idea spread.

Sabeer Bhatia was born in India in 1968. He came to the United States in 1988 to study at Caltech, and after graduation moved to Stanford to pursue graduate work. At Stanford, Sabeer attended brown-bag lunches where entrepreneurs such as Scott McNeally and Steve Jobs spoke and he caught the entrepreneurial bug.

Sabeer decided to take a job at Apple Computer and met Jack Smith, and together they moved to a startup called FirePower Systems. At FirePower Systems, Sabeer and Jack were working on cranking out processors used to help build PCs, but after two years the company wasn't doing much. The manager who had hired them had left the company, so they started looking around for new ideas.

The Internet was just beginning to blossom, and two of Sabeer's colleagues had some amazing success starting a little company called Yahoo, so they started working on a Web-based database that they called Javasoft. Sabeer and Jack put together a business plan and started to take it around to various venture capitalists, but they weren't getting very far. People kept asking them what their revenue model was. The truth was—other than advertising to the users of the service—they didn't have much. Advertising on the Internet was still a new idea and they were having trouble convincing anyone that it would really work.

Sabeer had an old e-mail account at Stanford and Jack had an AOL account, and each day they would dial into their e-mail accounts and exchange e-mails about their project. One day they came to work only to discover that the company had installed a new firewall. The firewall prevented them from dialing out and reaching their personal e-mail accounts. However, Jack and Sabeer could still reach any Website on the Internet, which made them ask, "What if we could access our e-mail from a Website?"

Sabeer and Jack realized that their new idea was much bigger than their original idea of creating a Web-based database system, but they felt that the original idea was more likely to get funding. They also realized that their idea was very simple and were worried about someone taking the idea. What would happen if they went to a venture capitalist who turned right around and told Netscape? After all, Netscape was just starting to build an e-mail system into their software. They were two hardware geeks with no management experience and no software experience. Who was going to fund them, anyway?

Torn between the two ideas, Sabeer and Jack continued to work full-time, and spent nights and weekends on the new product. Eventually, Sabeer (who was single and didn't have a lot of expenses) offered to give Jack half of his salary, so Jack could work full-time on the project. They planned to pitch the database idea and keep the e-mail idea in their back pocket until they found someone that they could trust.

Eventually, Draper Fisher Ventures invested $300,000 on the project. Sabeer and Jack decided to call their system HoTMaiL—the uppercase letters spell out HTML—and the new Web-based e-mail service launched on July 4, 1996.

In less than six months, the Website attracted more than 1 million subscribers. Within 30 months, Hotmail was the world's largest e-mail service, with more than 30 million active members. Just to put that number in perspective, Canada took 400 years to reach a population of 31 million people. That's a lot of people in a very short time.

Viral Marketing

The growth was so explosive that Draper Fisher Ventures invented a brand new term—*viral marketing*—to describe the growth experienced by Hotmail. The new term captures the nature of ideas that grow with the speed and unstoppable momentum of a cold virus. Imagine your own idea reaching that many people in a 30-month period. What would it take to duplicate Hotmail's numbers for your own idea?

The impact of Hotmail—as is the case with all things that affect millions of people—was a result of many different factors. Hotmail solved a real problem that millions of people were having. It was reliable, fast, and easy to use, and the idea itself was simple. People could grasp the idea instantly, which is a crucial factor in making ideas move rapidly and massively.

All of those factors are important if you want to achieve maximum impact, but the key element in Hotmail's success was a simple hyperlink at the bottom of each e-mail. The hyperlink advertises the service and invites you to tell your friends about it. Every e-mail sent out by the system increases the visibility and the number of users.

The key to any viral marketing is that you make it easy for people to spread the word. All that users had to do was send e-mails—something that they were already doing—and the rest happened automatically.

Viral marketing is really an Internet-enabled form of word-of-mouth marketing, which has been around for as long as mouths. What the Internet does is speed up the process, because now it is even easier and faster to spread the news about anything.

There are many things that we can do to speed the delivery of ideas, products, and services to our audience, but the first step is to create a solution that is built to spread. To make sure that your solution spreads, you need to:

- Solve a real problem.
- Keep the solution simple.
- Make it easy.

We need to spread the word quickly and massively. Luckily, there are key factors to help us spread the word more efficiently.

If You Want to Be Noticed, It Matters Who Hears You

K ey people are waiting to spread your message right now. They interact daily in networks that exist today where their influence is felt far beyond your limited vision of what you can do. If you know who to target and where to find the influencers, you can create a firestorm of activity around your project, before you even launch.

In *The Regis Touch: New Marketing Strategies for Uncertain Times,* Regis McKenna says, "90% of the world is influenced by the other 10%." If true, you can reach the entire world by reaching 10 percent of it. Let those key people influence the rest of the world. Now imagine that you take it another step. Use 10 percent of the influencers to influence the influencers. You want to make those key people your evangelists.

Many authors have talked about the key influencers and come up with terms to describe them and their common characteristics. The terms differ from author to author, but most of the ideas are similar. In this chapter we'll explore a number of these terms. As we talk about them, keep in mind that we are really talking about two things:

1. Networks of people.
2. Key influencers within the networks.

The important steps that we need to take are to:

- Identify the networks that our audience is currently a part of.
- Identify the key influencers within the networks.
- Motivate those key influencers to spread the word.

CHAPTER 9

Malcolm Gladwell, in *The Tipping Point,* talks about mavens, connectors, and salesmen.

Earlier, I mentioned my friend Blake, but one thing that I didn't mention is that he loves movies. Movies are one of the interests that Blake and I share, but when it comes to movies, there is a huge difference in our knowledge levels. Blake knows incredible mountains of information about any movie. In fact, eventually Blake sees almost every movie produced by a major motion picture studio, and many completely obscure films, too.

Blake is what Malcolm Gladwell would call a movie maven. Blake influences the movie-going habits of hundreds of people based solely on the fact that he knows so much about them. Whenever I have a question about a movie, I ask Blake. Whenever I am looking for a good movie to go watch, I ask Blake. After all, he's seen them all, and he cares enough about them to know what types of movies I might be interested in watching.

But it's not just me. Because of his position as the pastor of a good-sized church, Blake also has hundreds of other people who are aware of his specialized knowledge and come to Blake for movie advice. Now, I love movies, but no one is asking me which movies to go see. If I'm really impressed by a particular movie, I might tell someone, but that doesn't happen very often. On the other hand, people constantly ask Blake what movies are good, and he has some great advice that many people take.

There are many mavens in your life. Do automobile repairs challenge you? Maybe you know someone who knows cars extremely well you can ask. Who knows about gardening, pets, or any one of thousands of other subjects? Someone knows and, most likely, you know who that someone for you is.

Clearly, you have identified key people within your own networks who are mavens when it comes to particular subjects. So if you want to spread the word about your new movie, should you tell Blake or me?

Let's take a look at Malcolm's second key influencer. Do you know someone that just seems to know everyone? That person may be a connector.

Microsoft commissioned a study of the friendship patterns of more than 10,000 people in the UK and found that the average person in Britain has 33 friends. As we all know, not all friendships are equal. It's difficult to maintain very close relationships. Relationships take time, and there is only so much time in the world.

As it turns out, some people are very good at deep, close relationships. They typically have a very select group of close friends that they invest a lot of time in. If you are new to the neighborhood, this type of person is less likely to become your friend, because they have already invested in their current friends heavily. They simply don't have room for many friends. If you are this type of person, you may find yourself actually avoiding new relationships with people. Bottom line: You are booked.

Other people are very good at superficial relationships. They value people just as much as people who cultivate deep relationships do, but they crave bigger numbers. These people are much more comfortable maintaining contact with many people in a way that doesn't take up large amounts of their time. They aren't bothered by a lack of contact. In most cases, they are thrilled to revive contact after long absences. People who love to connect to many people are called connectors.

You've probably heard the term *six degrees of separation*. The term is part of a theory that everyone is no more than six "steps" away from any other person. A number of studies have attempted to verify this theory. It turns out, though less than six steps connect some people and more connect others, the number of steps is relatively small in almost every case.

Frigyes Karinthy was a Hungarian author who published a short story called "Chains," or "Chain-Links." The story is fiction, but it captured problems that people who study network theory wanted to explore. Karinthy thought that the world was shrinking as technology provided faster communications and easy travel. Networks could cover larger distances and friendships were possible in distant locations.

In the story, Karinthy's characters believe that any two individuals could connect through a maximum of five acquaintances. The idea took off in the form of a number of "small world" experiments, and, in 1967, researcher Stanley Milgram showed that on average people in the United States connected by approximately six friendship links.

What is interesting is some connectors keep cropping up all the time. If you were to flowchart out all of the connections between any groups of people, you would shortly discover that most of the connections travel through a select few individuals. Think about your life and you will be able to identify a few key connectors.

If you needed to find a plumber and didn't know anyone that knew about plumbing, who would you ask? Why does that person stand out in your mind? Maybe he or she doesn't know anything about plumbing, but he or she does know people. Find the people who know lots of people and you have a connector.

Malcolm Gladwell's final key influencer is the salesman. You'll have to ask Malcolm why he didn't use the word *salesperson*, but this one is easy. Everyone recognizes a good salesperson. Some people know how to persuade you to do anything. It may be their charm, their good looks, their intellect, but, whatever it is, they make you want to buy. If you want your ideas, products, and services to spread, you need salespeople to convince others that your ideas are worth having.

Seth Godin, best-selling author of *Unleashing the Ideavirus,* takes a little different route. Seth calls the key influencers "Sneezers." He even comes up with sub-types he calls "Promiscuous sneezers" and "Powerful sneezers."

You can easily persuade "Promiscuous sneezers" to spread your message. In fact, they will spread just about anyone's message. Unfortunately, because they spread many messages, they don't get a lot of respect. Don't let that discourage you. You want the maximum spread for your message, and "Promiscuous sneezers" are important to you.

"Powerful sneezers" are all about respect and trust. If they promote too many ideas, they lose power, so they are very selective about what they spread. When these people talk, other people listen, but it's much tougher to get them to talk about your ideas.

Emanuel Rosen, author of *The Anatomy of Buzz,* talks about Network Hubs and breaks the key influencers into media and non-media types. He calls the media types "Mega Hubs" and includes in that category people who are involved in the press, have a public role (politicians and celebrities, for example), or are acknowledged as experts.

No matter what you call the influencers, it's obvious that it matters who spreads your message. The real questions are: "How do you locate these key influencers?" and "How do you motivate them to spread the news?"

Let's talk about finding these people first. Luckily, most of these people are visible so it shouldn't be too difficult to find them. Also, while you are looking, keep in mind that these roles often overlap. Everyone has some characteristics of all of these role types. After all, we have to make sales every day, we need to connect with people every day, and we need to know things every day. It makes perfect sense that we all need to have at least some of these skills. What also makes perfect sense is that some of us are better at certain roles. Start looking for the best of the best.

Finding Key Influencers

One way to identify people is by their titles. Here are a few titles that key influencers may have chosen for themselves or been called by others:

Author	Executive
Expert	Millionaire
Reporter	Recognized authority
Guru	Champion
Professor	Administrator
Pastor	Boss
Politician	Leader
Celebrity	Ruler
Television host	Top dog
Producer	Mentor
Syndicated columnist	Coach
Professional	Knowledge broker
Teacher	Wizard
Artist	Instructor
Actor	Director
Writer	President
Television personality	Judge
Television anchor	Inventor
Magazine editor	Maven
Publisher	Professional
Kingpin	Scientist
Mastermind	Specialist
Pioneer	

A simple search can turn up amazing connections. Try combining some of these terms with the names of the networks you want to reach.

Let's say that you are interested in reaching the crafts niche. More specifically, you want to reach people who are interested in crafts that involve the use of paper. Trust me: I know nothing about paper crafts, so we are in this adventure together. If you do know something about paper crafts, then you are already way ahead of me.

First, let's do a search on Google. You can search on single words or phrases, or combine them to narrow down your search results. For now, let's search on the phrase "paper crafts" + expert. The quotation marks around the phrase *paper crafts* tells the search engine that I only want results that contain the exact phrase *paper crafts*. That will rule out many advertisements for paper of various types and other irrelevant links. The "+" tells the search engine to add the word expert to the search, so only pages that contain both the phrase *paper crafts* and the word *expert* will appear in the results.

We are looking for paper crafts experts and, sure enough, the first listing in the results links to a page on *expertvillage.com* that features thousands of how-to videos from experts in a wide range of specialties.

In the case of our search, the page shows us an expert that knows how to create "Tissue Paper Crafts." Other links take us to Web pages that showcase books, articles, or products. If you look closely, you will recognize that all of these pages lead us to people who fall into our key influencer categories.

Start making your lists now. Combine some of the terms in the list on page 135 and find your own words that describe the people that you are trying to reach. Each name on your list is a way to spread the word.

Let's go back to the math for a second. It's obvious that you want to reach the key influencers, but this could take a lot of time to do correctly. How can you reach key people efficiently? Let me give you an example from my own life.

As I told you earlier, my first big success was with a single influencer. Jim Daniels was what Seth Godin would call a "Powerful sneezer." Jim had 160,000 subscribers to sneeze at, and he didn't recommend a lot of products. Jim was as trustworthy as they come, and his subscribers believed what he said, so, when he told them to take action, they did. If you are trying to get your ideas out to your audience, then you want to look for people similar to Jim.

The Power of Joint Ventures

What Jim and I did together is typically called a joint venture, so let's talk about joint ventures for a few minutes. The basics of joint ventures are simple: Two people get together, share assets, and create something better than what they had when they started. In the case of marketing on the Internet, usually those assets take one of two forms: You have products to sell, or you have people who want to buy products.

Whether you are a product developer, a list owner, or just trying to reach a select group of people, you can't keep selling your audience the same products all the time. That is where the leveraged advantages of joint ventures come in.

Let's say for instance that I have a list and it has 50,000 people on it. Let's say that you have a list and it has another 50,000 people on it. The people on your list are not the same people on my list. That is where the advantage of joint ventures becomes very valuable. If I send my 50,000 people to buy a product that you might have to offer, and you send your 50,000 people to buy a product that I might have, then we're doubling our potential for profit with exactly the same number of assets.

What I've just described is really a form of barter. You advertise to your list, and I advertise to my list. We don't lose anything, and it doesn't cost us anything, but we double our profits. You can start to see that joint ventures can be powerful when used in the right way.

Okay, we've talked about the theory. Now let's just talk a little bit about how it works in the real world. Several years ago, I sent a simple e-mail to Jim Daniels. Jim is a world-famous Internet marketer who has been around for a long, long time.

Over time, Jim built up a list of probably 160,000 subscribers who know him, trust him, and listen to his opinions about new products and services. During the same period of time that Jim was building his list, I'd been working on the Internet slowly trying to build up my subscribers one at a time, trying to find people who would buy my products and services.

I had probably 2,000 people on my lists that I'd built up over a period of a year or two, and I decided whatever I was doing was not a very fast way to build up people. So I put on my thinking cap, and I finally realized that if I wanted to reach people I had to go to where they were. More importantly, if I wanted to talk to people and get them to buy my products and services, I needed to get somebody who they trusted to tell them that my products and services were worth what they'd have to pay for them.

Because I'd been reading Jim's newsletter, I decided I'd send him off a simple e-mail. Here's what I told Jim:

> "I've been working on products. I have some great software that I use to build portal sites and I think that you and I could work together and that we could put together something that would be of benefit to both of us."

Jim and I e-mailed back and forth. We shared ideas, we talked about possibilities for Websites, and eventually we came up with a system that we called Affiliate Showcase. Affiliate Showcase is a search engine and directory for affiliate programs, and it has a special twist.

You can insert your own affiliate links and your own affiliate programs into Affiliate Showcase, advertise your own version of Affiliate Showcase, and earn commissions from more than 3,000 programs in the system, plus you can add any program that you want to add. Affiliate Showcase gives you a place where you can promote multiple programs all from the same location.

After we had done our planning and some programming, and put together a beta program, we launched Affiliate Showcase. It almost immediately went into the top sites on the Internet! A large part of that success was because Jim Daniels was promoting Affiliate Showcase to his list. Since then, Affiliate Showcase has done hundreds and hundreds of thousands of dollars worth of business and has earned thousands of dollars for many individuals who have become Affiliate Showcase members.

All of this started from a simple e-mail, and all I did was approach somebody who already had contacts and who had trust built up already. I convinced Jim that I had quality services and products that we could work on together, and leveraged his people and my products so that we could make something that was even bigger than what Jim or I had separately.

I could go on and on about all of the joint ventures that I've participated in since then. My membership site, *jvAlert.com,* is all about creating successful joint ventures, and jvAlert itself is the result of a joint venture that Sid Hale and I put together, but it never would have happened if we hadn't created our relationship by working together at *AffiliateShowcase.com.*

Now, I have joint ventures growing out of joint ventures—all of the people who have joined *jvAlert.com* are becoming partners with me in all kinds of different projects—so it just grows and grows. That's impact.

So, the next questions are: "How do you get started in this? How do you take all the ideas, products, services and resources that you have and leverage them to make your impact grow with joint ventures?"

Before You Start

There are a few things that you want to think about before you even start to go out and approach somebody about a joint venture:

- What the short- and long-term goals of your venture are.
- What kinds of deals you want to get involved in.
- What you should offer and what you should not offer.
- What people will accept and what they won't accept in a joint venture offer.
- Who is going to have what responsibilities.
- Who is going to own any products that you may jointly produce.
- Who has the copyright and how the income and expenses get split.

If you know—before you start—exactly what you want to get out of a joint venture, you'll have a lot better luck convincing somebody else to agree to your terms. The one thing that we do know is that we want to make this a win-win situation. So look at this from the other person's side for just a couple of minutes.

What kinds of relationships do people like to get involved in, and what do you think will work for them? Imagine just for a second that you are that high-powered, top-level affiliate, or top-level Internet marketer—what types of things would you be looking for?

Well, I think one thing for sure would be that you would want to have something that is going to generate a reasonable amount of impact or profit for not too much effort on your part. So visibility, ease of use, and dollar volume always seem to come into play on these types of arrangements. Let's face it: We're all lazy, and the easier that you can make things for someone the more chance you have of convincing him or her of working with you. Secondly, let's remember that top-level marketers are getting dozens of joint venture proposals almost every day. You really need to make yours stand out.

Finding Your Partners

The next question becomes: "How do you find people to partner with who are going to be top-level and give your ideas, products, and services the most exposure?" Or, if you sit on the other side of the equation: "How do you find high-quality products and services that you can promote and make the highest possible revenues from? With thousands and thousands of marketers trying to get your attention, how do you know which ones are successful?"

One of the places to start is *Alexa.com*. Alexa is a site that gathers Internet information and has a toolbar that people can download to tell how much traffic a particular site is going to receive, or has received in the past. This toolbar is not an exact representation of exactly how much traffic people get, but it is a representation of how many people who have actually downloaded this Alexa toolbar have gone to a particular site.

What Alexa does is rank sites from the most-visited sites on the Internet down to people that get almost no traffic at all. They give you a rating for that particular site, and you can even get traffic details that will show you over time what a particular site has done. So, does this mean if the site is rated number 2,000 in terms of traffic ranking that they really are in the top 2,000 sites on the Internet in terms of the traffic? Not necessarily, but it's an indication of a site that gets at least some traffic to it, and by comparing sites and their Alexa ratings you can tell whether or not people are going to a particular site on a regular basis.

High Alexa rankings—and by that I mean the lower numbers—generally indicate that a Website has traffic, and traffic is one of the criteria that you want to look for when you're looking for a partner. Notice I say it's only one of the criteria. Many sites have traffic, but haven't really built up a level of trust with the people that go to their site.

You can generate a lot of traffic by buying co-registration leads or by buying advertising, but you haven't really built up a relationship with that audience until there is an interaction that's back and forth between you and the potential customer: You give them some sort of value, and they learn to trust you and your opinion on things.

Trust is a huge factor in determining whether you'll purchase eventually from the person or company that is associated with a particular Website. Some people have built up this trust over years and years and years, and you can capitalize on that.

Who Do the People Trust?

So how do you know who's built up trust? First, look at the people that you trust:

- What newsletters do you subscribe to?
- Who do you know is a reliable source for information?
- What Websites do you find that are great resources for the type of people you want to attract?
- Where will those people be going, and who will they be listening to?

When I started *jvAlert.com,* I knew that I wanted to reach the top marketers in the world. The first thing that I did was subscribe to every single newsletter that I could possibly find. There are a number of quality directories of ezines and newsletters. If you go to *AffiliateShowcase.com* and put "ezine" in the search engine, you'll get a list of all kinds of resources that you can use to locate publishers of ezines.

If you subscribe to all kinds of ezines, what do you get over a period of time?

Well, very quickly, you:

- Get a sense of who you can trust and who you can't trust.
- Get a sense of the people who put out quality work and the people who don't.
- Know who is just putting out hype.

I talked to my girls when they were growing up about liars. I told them, "You may not be able to catch somebody in a lie, but, over time, you usually know who the liars are." The same holds true when you're reading someone's work over a period of time. My guess is that you're not going to buy from a liar and you aren't going to buy from somebody who just produces hype. That's not the type of person that you're going to want to partner with. You can recognize quality and so can your potential customers.

The Importance of Quality

The main point is to always deal with quality. So you've gone out and you've identified all kinds of publications and all kinds of Internet marketers. You can grab even more if you just look for search terms such as *Internet marketing guru*. You'll find lists of people who you may or may not want to partner with. Pretty soon, you develop a sense of who has high visibility in the marketplace. Does this mean they're the best people to market with? Absolutely not. What you need to do is find people who recommend quality products to the types of markets that you want to reach.

I want to encourage you to do this right. Take the time that it takes to build relationships with people who will be effective at marketing your products and services and partnering with you. Long before you approach somebody with a joint venture offer, subscribe to his or her newsletter. Spend some time looking at exactly what they're saying and taking it all in. Build a dialogue with them—don't make the first words out of your mouth "this is what I can do for you" or "this is what you can do for me."

Building the Relationship

Every Internet marketer on the face of the earth has seen e-mails that start out with "Boy, I really enjoyed your article" or "I'm sitting here right now at your Website, and I really like what you're doing. I think that this is the perfect opportunity for me to help you out." Guess what. Immediately that first reaction is: "What are you trying to sell me?" If you've seen it in a form letter, you know that the marketer has seen the same thing thousands of times.

So what can you really do to build a relationship? Make honest comments on the work that they're doing. Ask questions—get a dialogue going. Make this thing two-way, and do it without asking for anything. Then just let some time go by. It's really hard to believe, but there are people on the other side of the e-mail—they're human the same as everybody else. They have wants and desires, they have friends, they have wives and children—lots of things that you can talk about besides just making a buck.

Now, I can hear you thinking right now, "But I haven't got that kind of time—I don't want to waste time trying to build up relationships with people when I need thousands of people to come to my site, and I need it to happen right now." Part of the reason that we put together jvAlert was to help people do exactly that—to build relationships with people who they hadn't had any contact with and to know that you are only dealing with quality people that are serious Internet marketers.

Lessons From jvAlert

What Sid Hale and I did when we first started jvAlert was to go out to people who we knew and we trusted, and we invited them to come in and join us in a very, very select group where they would know that they were only working with top-level people. Then we asked them: "Who do you respect? Who do you like to deal with? Who are the top people that you would recommend?"

We opened up the group to people who received invitations from our members. The people who got invitations were the people that top marketers thought were the best in the world. Next, we started testing the system.

The system really consists of a very, very specialized search engine that puts together resources from top-level marketers and matches them with joint venture offers.

Because the members of jvAlert know that they're only dealing with top-quality people, they're willing to give better commissions and better deals than they would ordinarily in the public marketplace. This data system has run along really well for a long time. We built up a very, very tight-knit group of people who were top, top quality, and we still hadn't really invited the public at large into jvAlert.

After we worked out all the kinks and bugs, and fine-tuned the system and made it even more powerful, we decided that we would start the launch. We allowed our members to invite anybody that they wanted into the membership of jvAlert. Almost instantly, *jvAlert.com* went to the top of the charts at Alexa.com for the traffic rankings. People were moving to jvAlert in record numbers, we were generating all kinds of traffic, and suddenly we had new members all over the place.

The new members and traffic generated many joint venture offers. But, did that make the resource more useful? Well, not immediately.

First, people had to learn how to do joint venture offers that worked. The quality of the joint venture offers at jvAlert was the real drawing card for the members there, and suddenly the quality of the offers was slipping. The first thing that we did was to put in a manual review system of all of the offers to make sure that the quality of the offers was as high as what our members had been experiencing before we let everybody in.

Secondly, we began a process of educating people. We really needed to teach them how to negotiate joint venture offers that would stand out above the crowd, that would be something special. So how do you do that? Well, the first thing that you need to realize is that if you're going to go in and just offer the same thing that you offer to everybody else to a top-level marketer, you're not going to get very far.

So, if you go to a top-level marketer and say, "Look, I've got this great product, and I'll pay you a 10 percent commission on it," you're going to get absolutely zero. The next thing that people wanted to do was to just say, "Okay, well, I'll give more commission. So let's make this a 50 percent commission or a 75 percent commission and people will jump all over this."

What Else Can You Do?

Well, most people probably would jump all over a 75 percent commission, but if you're a top-level marketer you're looking for something a little different. Sure, you want the high level of commission, but you want something extra in addition to that.

One of the things that you need to realize is that high-level marketers generally only have so many opportunities to promote. You can't keep promoting over and over to the same list with the same products or the same types of products, and expect response to continue in the way that you would like it to.

What you have to do is handpick products that match exactly the type of clients that you're working with and that have extremely high value for them. Then you have to give them something extra to make it even more enticing to them.

Why not add another product to your offer? Don't be satisfied with a single offer: Give them some bonus to give away, give their members an extra discount, offer to promote one of their products to your list, give them a related article to publish in their newsletter, or offer to combine your products with some of theirs.

Remember that joint ventures don't have to be just between two people—lots of people can join in your joint venture, and sometimes the more the merrier. Once you get one top-level marketer to join your joint venture, go out looking for some more. You can use the participation of your first marketer to encourage other marketers to join in. It will give you a sense of credibility and a sense of value for other top-level marketers.

In general, top-level marketers are looking for either high levels of commissions, meaning high-dollar values, or recurring commissions, which also over time equals high-dollar values because they have limited numbers of slots that they can promote in. The other thing that all marketers are interested in is visibility.

One great way to produce a high-dollar volume and high quality at the same time is to combine multiple products into the same package.

Start with your contribution, then capture your first high-level marketer and ask him or her to add his or her product to the list. Then go to a series of other marketers and see if they will add theirs to the package. What you can end up with is a great product, a great value, and a large number of people who are all promoting your product.

E-mail may be the fastest way to reach someone, but it's not necessarily the best way to build a relationship. In most cases, you can get a sense of a person much more easily and faster using the telephone. Believe me: I know how you feel about using that telephone, but drop somebody an e-mail and ask: "What's a good time to call?" Then, when he or she responds back to your e-mail, you already have an invitation to give him or her a call—and you've started to build a relationship.

Remember that you don't have to make that phone call to say, "Buy this; work this deal with me." Just meet the person, ask a few questions about his or her business, explore some of the possibilities that he or she has, and ask about his or her products and services. You know he or she will be happy to tell you about that. You can expand from there. Take a look at all the possibilities. See how he or she can work with you and your business. You'll get a sense of what he or she is doing, what types of things he or she is looking for, and how the two of you can work best together.

Throughout this whole process, keep in mind that it has to be win-win.

You have to both benefit from a joint venture relationship, or it's just not worth it. The key skill that you need when negotiating a joint venture is to actually listen to the other person so that you can make it valuable to him or her and hear what his or her potential problems are.

Having Joint Venture Success the Easy Way

Here are 10 easy steps to joint venture success:

1. **Define your goals.**

   If you don't know what you want to achieve in the first place, how are you ever going to get there? Don't forget to include both long-term and short-term goals. Make the short-term goals little steps towards what you want to get to eventually. Know what kind of a deal you want to make; know what kind of profits you want to make out of that deal; know how much time you're willing to put into it and what results you expect to get out of it. If the deal that you come up with doesn't meet your goals, scrap it and start over again.

2. **Make the key ownership decision.**

   Who owns what, is important. And while you're thinking about ownership, remember that with ownership comes liability. Who's going to be responsible when this thing doesn't work out the way that you think it will? In almost every case, the person that has ownership also has the greatest liability. So make sure you're covered for that.

3. **Get the responsibilities right.**

   Make sure you know exactly who is going to do what, make sure you know when they're going to do it, and make sure that you know what happens when they don't.

4. **Create deals that people want to participate in.**

   That goes back to the win-win situation that we were talking about before. Make sure that you're offering something of value. Make sure that they make money off of it, and you'll have repeat joint ventures that will do even more. Be creative. People are looking for deals that are new and different.

5. **Find top-level partners.**

   You want to do this right, so take your time. Go out and find people who you trust; find people who you know and respect, and who others will, too.

6. **Write an irresistible offer.**

   Make this something that's going to stand out in the crowd, and then put it down on paper—not so you're locked into it, but so that you have something to work from that clearly expresses what goals you've set up and meets them, but is still flexible enough to be adapted for any marketer that you might come across.

7. **Negotiate a winning deal.**

   That's back to the win-win again, but this time you want to make sure your behind is covered and that your goals are met. There is no need to give away the whole farm. What you need to do is meet the needs of the person who you're dealing with. Listen to him or her and find out what goals he or she wants to meet; make sure that you meet those goals, and make sure that you meet yours at the same time. Remember that anything that you don't give away is money in your pocket.

8. **Make sure it happens.**

   An incredibly high percentage of deals that have been discussed, negotiated, and all set up, never happen—and usually the reason is just simple follow-up. People's lives are busy. They get distracted. They do other things. Just make sure that it happens. Consistently follow up with your partner. Make sure he or she is still on the same page. Make sure that he or she is meeting the goals and the responsibilities that he or she agreed to meet, then do the same thing for yourself. Make sure that you have a list of exactly what you've agreed to do and then step through that list, one step at a time, making sure that everything you agreed to do, you actually do.

9. **Double your profits by tracking your results.**

   So many times, we leave out this aspect, and it needs to be set up in advance. You need to know where every sale comes from. You need to know what resources you use to get them and how much they cost, both in time and money.

10. **Calculate a return on investment for a joint venture.**

    Here's how:

    ☐ Put a dollar value on your time.

    ☐ Calculate the total investment for each marketing possibility. That's the time, multiplied by the value of your time, plus any cash required, and that equals your investment.

    ☐ Estimate the number of sales or sign-ups from each marketing possibility.

    ☐ Divide the total investment by the estimated sign-ups or sales.

    ☐ Rank those by the return on investment.

As you go on, test, test, test, and retest to see where you're actually producing the results and then re-rank your list. That way you know which joint ventures are actually working for you, what they are taking up of your time and resources, and what the return on investment you're getting actually is.

The bottom line is that you want to invest more time and effort into the techniques that are working for you in actual practice. Also, you want to identify the areas that might not be worth your hourly rate, but that may be worth someone's hourly rate.

Repetitive tasks may not be your cup of tea, but you may find areas that pay off big time that are just a matter of putting in time. You may not have the time but, if it makes money, you can find resources that may pay off for you when you outsource repetitive tasks that generate income.

Joint ventures are a great way to find those resources. Or maybe you are on the opposite side of that: Maybe you have lots of time and not so many resources. Time is a great resource to use in a negotiation for a joint venture. If you have lots of it, it's a great commodity to bargain with.

Do it all again. Once you've gone through the process, you've developed a great set of resources. You already know some of the people—you have partners, and you've built relationships. Now all you have to do is leverage those resources repeatedly.

Exponential Results

Now let's talk about a couple of ways to produce exponential joint venture results.

The first thing to remember is that endorsements always work better than advertising. If someone who people know and trust is recommending an idea, product, or service, then results are going to be exponentially higher. If endorsements are detailed and enthusiastic, they always work better than short, little blurbs. Endorsements that are made by people who endorse relatively few products work better than people endorsing your product that endorse other products every day.

Generally, the more endorsements that you have the better they work, but that's not always the case. A very personalized endorsement will always work better than something that reads as if it's a form letter.

As consumers, we want to know that we aren't being ripped off. We want to know that people are offering genuine value for the hard-earned cash that we give them. That's why personalized endorsements always work better than ordinary advertising.

Now, don't get me wrong. Advertising works.

The question with advertising is: What is the price that we can get that advertising for?

The nice thing about advertising is that you can usually get more of it. So if you can get into a situation in which you can routinely generate the same profits over and over and over again, advertising can make those exponential profits just by increasing the amount of advertising that you do.

The nice thing about joint ventures is that we can work advertising angles, product angles, and personalized endorsements all at the same time. The effect will be exponential, too. Why stick with just one thing? The more possibilities we combine, the bigger the result.

Another way that we can exponentially increase our joint venture results is to concentrate on the back end. Many times, we don't have the time or resources to build products and services that are complimentary to the ones that we already have.

If you can joint venture with someone who already has those products or services, you can create exponential profits just by offering their products to an already-eager audience who is interested in a particular line of products or services. Many times, you can use a low price item to sell an even higher priced item, which creates even more revenue.

Watching Out for Mistakes

So what kinds of mistakes can you make? The sky is the limit. You have to watch out for the potholes—that's for sure—and you need to protect yourself.

Legal and accounting issues can hurt you big time, so you need to know what the liabilities are and what the responsibilities are, and you have to know who the ownership sits with.

First, you need to know what form your agreement is going to take:

- Is it just a contract?
- Is it a partnership?
- Do you form a new corporation?

A formal corporation may offer the benefit of limited shareholder liability, but many times contracts require personal liability. A partnership can even be scarier with the prospect of unlimited liability for all the partners with the result that limited liability can be more of a myth than a reality.

Also, with a more formalized joint venture, there is the added cost of setting up and maintaining the accounting expenses for those structures that you've created. Most often, some type of a contract is used that allows the parties to separate their respective contributions, and there is some flexibility to actually sharing responsibilities and whether or not you carry out your own part, or what expenses you may be able to write off in the joint venture.

Also, don't forget the taxman when you set up the form for your joint venture. Eventually, you're going to have to pay on any profits that you may produce.

You also want to look at how you dissolve the relationship:

- When is the relationship over?

- How can you get out of the agreement, and what consequences result from that?

☐ ☐ ☐

If you plan correctly and think about potential problems before you start, you've ruled out a lot of problems.

Now you've got all of these complexities going on in your mind, and you're wondering how you could possibly do this and still make it work. Is it really worth all the effort, the time, and the planning and the building of relationships to create a joint venture? The answer is absolutely.

What Do You Have to Offer?

Feeling as though you don't have much to contribute to a joint venture relationship?

What if you don't have 50,000 people on your list?

What if you don't have a great product?

What if you don't have a lot of money?

The truth is that as human beings we all have something to offer. Usually the first things that pop into your mind when you start a project are that it takes either time or money, and usually both. The "usually both" is where you come in.

If you don't have time, maybe you have money. It certainly helps to have both and sometimes it's easier to put two people together to get both aspects of this relationship.

Maybe you don't have time, and maybe somebody else does. If you can work with that person, it makes it a lot easier for you to reach your goals.

If you have a lot of time, but you don't have much money, maybe you can find somebody who has something of value that you can spend time on to produce more profits for both of you.

Don't underestimate creativity. Ideas may be a dime a dozen, but good ideas are worth something. All that you need to do is combine your good ideas together with the assets to make them happen.

The biggest asset you have is the ability to make something happen—to actually follow through on it and see that something is done. That particular trait is so rare that true innovators jump all over it the second that they see it. If I meet somebody who can actually get something done, who actually follows through on what he or she is promising and who does what he or she says that he or she will do, it's a great value to me as a marketer.

You can develop honesty, reliability, sincerity, and the ability to get things done, and you can sell them as assets. If you produce, people will come back repeatedly to create more joint ventures with you.

I wish that joint venturing were more difficult, more complex, more secret. Just think of all the things that I could sell you. But the truth is that joint venturing is all about building relationships one little step at a time—person to person. It's getting to know them, building piece-by-piece the little things that make a friendship, and then using those assets that both of you have naturally to come up with ideas, with projects and with exponential results from your efforts.

Here are the basics again:

First, put together your ideas.

- Know what your goals are.

- Think about what you want to do and how you want to achieve your goals.

- Think about what you want to give up and what you don't want to give up.

- Plan for the future.

Then concentrate on locating people who can help with your projects. Use the available tools to find out who's trusted. Who has an audience that listens to what they are saying, that they respect, and that you can trust?

- Build relationships with those people one step at a time—one simple phone call—one idea tossed back and forth between two people.

- Don't push. Simply explore the possibilities. Build the relationship before you try to make a deal.

- Listen to what people have to say.

- Respond to their needs and try to find situations in which both of you can win.

- When you find those situations, make sure that you meet your partner's needs and your needs, and when you've done that—stop. There is no need to give away the farm, but you do need to make sure that everybody wins.

- Hammer out all of the responsibilities. Find out who has the ownership and who has the liabilities. Then check those situations and find the best form that you possibly can for this joint venture.

- Build your joint venture so that it produces exponential profits.

- Combine with other joint ventures, work with other partners, make something even bigger.

Don't forget the back end. Many times profits can be much higher on the back end then your original sale, and joint venture partners can help you to build bigger and more profitable products by combining resources, by combining promotional attempts and by combining products to make something even better. I'll tell you a few more tricks of the trade soon!

The first key to joint venture success is finding key people to joint venture with who can enhance your ideas, products, and services. The second is building relationships with those people, and the third is motivating those people to take action.

But, wouldn't it be nice if things just happened automatically? Well, it just so happens that there are many ways to make your impact spread without taking constant action yourself. What if you created your own system, and it took off as if it were an Ebola virus? So let's...

Make It Contagious: Spread Your Ideas Automatically

T ime is limited, so we need to make sure that you get your message out as quickly and automatically as a virus spreads in the middle of an epidemic. The impact that you create today needs to replicate quickly and abundantly, and it must live long enough to exponentially grow before it fades out of sight.

Here's the difference between incremental and exponential results. Let's say that you are trying to build an audience and add prospects for your latest idea.

Incremental	Exponential
□ Add one prospect every day □ In 30 days you have 30 prospects	□ Double your prospects every day □ In 30 days you have 536,870,912 prospects

Sounds good, right? Then reality kicks in.

Try this little bit of exponential origami:

- Take a sheet of paper.
- Fold it in half.
- Fold it a second time.
- Fold it a third time.
- Continue folding for as long as you can.

CHAPTER 10

By the time that you get it folded seven times, it's about the thickness of a notebook. Most people give up at this point, but, if you are persistent, at 10 times it's about the width of your hand. It's only physically possible to do it about 12 times, but if you could keep folding it:

- 17 times: is taller than the average house.
- 60 times: has the diameter of the known solar system.
- 100 times: has the radius of the universe.

If you don't believe me, go to *TheImpactFactor.com/resources*, and I'll give you the math.

The thing that you have to remember about exponential results is that it usually gets harder each time that you double something. In fact, there are physical restraints and marketing restraints. You can't fold the paper more than 12 times, and you can't grow your prospect list larger than the number of people in the market. People who run pyramid schemes have tried it, and it just doesn't work.

What does work is to identify things that can grow exponentially and focus on how to grow them automatically. After all, if you want to double the number of prospects that you currently have, all you need to do is to get your prospects to bring in new prospects faster than you lose the old ones. In other words, if you go out and get 10 prospects, you have...10 prospects. If you get 10 prospects and all of your prospects consistently go out and get you more prospects, then you can have exponential growth. Note: Prospects have many more opportunities to bring in prospects than you do.

Here's how it works in the real world. Just think about the growth of Hotmail. Each customer that sends out an e-mail also sends out a link that enables the recipient of the e-mail to sign-up for the service. At least at the start, more people signed up than canceled their accounts, therefore the service grew like crazy. Eventually things leveled off, but, while there was market to claim, Hotmail did a good job of claiming it.

Integrate Your Ideas.

You don't have to stop with automating your own systems for spreading your message. How would you like to integrate your messages into the marketing of your clients, customers, partners, and even competitors? You can integrate your content, products, and lead generation systems into all of them.

Mark Joyner talks about the example of a small software company that had acquired some useful software from another company. A computer hardware company thought the software would be perfect for their computer. Ordinarily, a hardware company would just purchase the rights to use the software on their computers. In this case, the software company did offer to license the software, but they retained the rights to offer the software to other hardware manufacturers.

What the software company was doing was integrating their software into the computer company's system. Instantly, the software company had a huge client base. They didn't have to go out and find those new customers, or spend hundreds of thousands or even millions building those relationships. They borrowed all of the credibility of the computer company and ended up with a total integration of their software product into the computer.

Even better, they were free to go to another company and do exactly the same thing repeatedly. In case you were wondering, it turned out well for the small software company. Microsoft went on to make billions from integrating their software into countless computers. A large part of that success was because of the customer base that they built by automatically being integrated into other companies' products.

Of course, you don't have to integrate deeply to get your message out—although you really should explore all of the options. Here are a few places you can integrate your message into other people's Websites, products, services, and other systems:

- Order pages
- Subscription conformation pages
- Logout pages
- Autoresponder e-mails
- Membership areas
- Physical products
- Exit popup windows
- Co-op advertising
- Inserts in mailings
- Live event gift packages
- Sponsorships

The key is to make it as easy on your partners as possible, and that means automating the process as much as you can. Don't expect a partner to do custom programming to integrate your system into theirs. A skilled programmer can help you to set up a system that will allow your partners to integrate your entire system into any Website with a couple of lines of code.

Beyond the Message

Automation can be amazing, and it doesn't just stop at spreading your message. Here are just a few things that you can automate to save time and keep your growing impact in motion:

- Accounting
- Affiliate payments
- Backups
- Bank deposits
- Blog entries
- Competition analysis
- Customer service
- E-mail management
- Fax broadcasts
- Forum postings
- Getting testimonials
- Partner recruitment
- Phone systems
- Referrals
- Sales force
- Sales reports
- Signups

About this time, you might start thinking, "There you go again. Ken, you must be nuts! I'm just one person, and I don't have time to deal with automating all that!" We all think that way sometimes, but we both know that you don't have enough time, and that means automation is crucial to your continued sanity. The choice is automate or waste time, and, if you choose to waste time, you won't reach your maximum impact. After reading this far, that's just not an option.

Automate This?

The real question is what you should automate and what you should not automate.

Let's say that you are running a business. You are advertising and selling widgets. Your competitor is selling exactly the same widget at a slightly higher price and processing the same number of orders.

There are more orders out there. In fact, your customers will buy as many widgets as you can produce. The problem is that your production is manual and you can only produce 100 widgets a day.

Here are your current numbers:

Number of Sales:	100
Price of Product:	$295
Total Sales:	$29,500

Meanwhile, here are your competitor's numbers:

Number of Sales:	100
Price of Product:	$395
Total Sales:	$39,500

You realize that you can automate the process and be able to produce twice as many widgets in half the time. If you do, here's how your numbers will look:

Number of Sales:	400
Price of Product:	$295
Total Sales:	$118,000

Now that's a great reason to automate, right?

Well, not necessarily. Unfortunately, you aren't making a profit. For each sale that you make, you are losing 10 dollars. How do you like those numbers? What you have effectively done is quadrupled your losses. If something isn't working, making that process more efficient doesn't help. The first rule of automation is this:

> "Don't automate things that aren't working."
>
> —Ken McArthur

What we want to do is automate things that are already working well. My recommendation is you first do all processes manually. Just dive right in and do the work. Then when you absolutely understand the process, have fine-tuned it so that it just hums along like clockwork, and you know that it's not likely to change any time soon, then automate it. Start with the processes that will have the most impact on your goals.

Let's say you have a wonderful computer. It's the latest processor, has this incredibly fast hard drive and a wonderful flat screen monitor that is huge, and has great color. It interfaces with a ton of the latest high-tech equipment, and you have all of the latest software on it. You sit down to crank out some insights and genuine wisdom to your audience and the hard drive dies.

Your entire computer system is dependent on that one piece of hardware. So that tells you that it's a crucial element. If your hard drive doesn't work, you are out of a computer. In the same way, if you don't generate audience, you are out of the impact business. What are the crucial processes that will not allow you to operate if they break down?

Your hard drive is useless by itself. Can you imagine a computer system that is only a hard drive? Well, maybe you can, but it certainly doesn't do much. How can you compute anything if your computer doesn't have a processor? How can you see anything if your computer doesn't have a monitor?

So if you only have an audience, then you aren't going to have much impact. You need to have a solution to a problem and a way to deliver that solution. You need to have systems in place to communicate with that audience. The list goes on, but you get the idea. Nothing stands alone.

The message can come and go. Maybe the message is one thing today, and next week you have a completely new message, but, if you build a system, then you can always deliver the message no matter what message you are delivering today. The media can change, the message can change, the back-end products and services can change, but a system will work forever. More about that soon.

It doesn't matter whether your personal impact goal is to make a million dollars or cure cancer. Here are three core systems to consider:

1. Marketing
2. Sales
3. Support

You can automate all of these systems. What you need to do is figure out which one will have the greatest impact—that you can control.

> "If you can't control it, why waste time on it?"
>
> —Ken McArthur

Let's face it: We can't control everything. In fact, there are lots of things that we have very little control over. I don't have personal control over whether or not my country decides to go to war. If a war does break out, it will certainly have a huge impact on my life. I can take a stab at trying to elect the right leaders or to influence the discussions, but bottom line: I'm not in control of whether my country goes to war. What's more, there are plenty of things that I can control, so it's a better use of my time to focus on those tasks.

In fact, I can improve tons of things. You see, if we start looking at the key processes, you will see room for improvement almost everywhere—and you're right: You can't fix them all at once. The key is to focus on a single issue. I suggest that you focus on one of the three systems I mentioned. Even better, identify a single process within that system and focus all of your energy on that one process until you nail it.

Which process? These questions are time versus value equations, so you need to look at your systems from both perspectives. Where are you spending most of your time? Where are you getting the most value in terms of things that move you directly towards meeting your goals?

Ask yourself what activities you should do personally.

As my business grew, I found that customer support was eating up hours each day of my personal time. My first attempt at fixing the problem was to put up a forum and send people to the forum for customer support. We had a group of supportive people to answer questions on the forum, and that helped to take off some of the load.

Unfortunately, some questions involved payments or required access to membership files, so my next step was to hire a local person to come to my house each day for four hours. Although the person I hired showed up each day and did what I asked him to do, the truth was he wasn't very savvy about computers in general and even less so about marketing online. Although the work was being done, it wasn't the best possible system.

My next attempt was to install a help desk system. The help desk system allows clients to receive fast and efficient answers for their questions. The system automatically searches through previous answers to questions and suggests responses when a client asks a question. If they don't find their answer in the previous issues, clients can submit a new question from any online browser. Immediately, my customer support team gets an e-mail notification (on their PDA if desired) or can simply log in from any online browser to work on issues in their category of expertise. That means that customer service people can be mobile and still have all the tools they need to provide excellent customer support. It also means that they don't have to live in my neighborhood or come to my basement to work.

Because customer service was eating up lots of my personal time, it was a key focus point for my business at the time. Once you get one process working optimally, you can move onto the next process.

The key is to focus on a single issue, because multi-tasking can kill your productivity. We think we are good at multi-tasking, but the truth is that we are awful at it. That's because we get charged a "resumption tax"—from a couple of seconds up to hours of lost time—every time you try to restart your original task and get back on track again. Each time you switch tasks, the "resumption tax" kicks in again, and the time really adds up. If you aren't doing something that contributes to your key process, then you are wasting time.

You need that time, because, now that you have clear ideas, your own unique story, key influencers plus integrated products and services, you are ready to build a...

Pressure Cooker: How to Launch Like a Steaming Hot Fire Hose

N ow it's time to create a pressure cooker, build intensity, and finally explode at the precise moment for maximum results—while you create your own starving crowd, begging for everything that you have to offer.

To have a successful launch, you need to start planning early. You need to know your goals, what assets you have, the key elements required for success, and the best launch strategy to follow for maximum impact. You need to build prospect lists, products, partners, sales copy, a Website, a support system, and a launch team. Don't worry if you don't know how to do these things; visit *TheImpactFactor.com/resources/* for more free resources. You are going to want to know how to do all of these things and more. After all, you are…

Going for a Blockbuster!

Blockbuster was originally a term coined by the press during World War II to describe a bomb big enough to destroy an entire city block. In the early 1950s, the Hollywood press began to use it in the movie industry to describe large movie productions or high box office receipts. Of course, large productions don't always mean high box office receipts. The movie industry is full of expensive productions that failed miserably at the box office.

Budget has always played a role in the ways studios produce and promote movies. In the 1940s and '50s, a motion picture with a low budget was usually used as the bottom half of a double feature.

Those movies were called "B" movies and were less-publicized than their high-budget companions, By the end of the 1950s, production of movies designed as second features had largely died out.

From about 1948 until 1974, the movie industry was in a slump. Box office receipts and profits were both down. Finally, the industry pulled out of the slump by financing the "auteur renaissance," a movement that backed powerful directors such as Martin Scorsese, Robert Altman, Stanley Kubrick, William Friedkin, Peter Bogdanovich, and Terrence Malick. It was a temporary measure. The trend that changed the movie industry forever happened in the mid-1970s with the release of *Jaws* in 1975 and *Star Wars* in 1977.

These movies changed the way that movie studios produced, promoted, and distributed their movies and produced almost unbelievable profits for the studios. The movies also influenced the entire culture at the same time. That's impact.

In movie theaters, films have a limited shelf life that lasts from as little as a week to as much as six months. The timing of movie marketing is crucial because you have to get audiences out of their houses and into the cinemas at exactly the right time. Once that time has past, you are out of luck. Starting with *Jaws,* Stephen Spielberg created the "summer block-buster" format and almost single-handedly created a shift towards "event marketing" that continues to this day. As the term *event marketing* implies, with this type of promotion the launch of the movie becomes an "event" and the event becomes the focus of the marketing.

The Laws of Influence

Event marketing often relies on some basic laws of influence Robert B. Cialdini, author of *Influence: the Psychology of Persuasion,* developed and tested. Cialdini indentifies six key "weapons" that can be used to influence others. You want to keep the following influence factors in mind as you plan your blockbuster launch:

- Reciprocity
- Commitment and consistency
- Social proof
- Authority
- Liking
- Scarcity

Reciprocity

Reciprocity is the tendency to want to return a favor. If I do something for you, the natural urge is for you to want to do something for me. We don't like relationships to be one-sided, and we don't enjoy being in debt to someone. In fact, if you do something for someone, he or she feels almost completely bound to reciprocate in some way. Even if you don't accept a gift, you often feel responsible to be giving in return. Reciprocity is the reason that we receive so many offers of free samples.

Commitment and Consistency

If you say you are going to do something, you feel committed to do it. Sometimes when someone tries to sell you an expensive item, he or she asks you to commit to the sale based on certain conditions. For instance, "If I can get you another $500 off, would you agree to purchase this item today?" In this case, let's say that you agree, and the salesperson comes back after talking to the manager and says that the reduced price isn't available. Do you still buy? As it turns out—even if he or she removes the incentive—you are more likely to make the purchase, because you feel that you committed to it.

Social Proof

People want assurance they are doing the right thing. One of the ways that they get assurance is to observe what other people are doing. If everyone else is doing the same thing, we feel as though we must be right, too. The truth is that people often do the wrong thing en masse, but on average we are more likely to survive if we agree with the crowd, so it's built right into our system. We always check and see what the masses think. Do you want to get someone to stare up into the sky? All you need to do is gaze into the sky. Before you know it, people will be doing what you do. As the crowd grows, more people will look up. If you found a crowd of 50 people looking up in the sky, wouldn't you look?

Authority

The Milgram experiments in the early 1960s proved that people would do horrible things to each other simply because someone in authority told them that they should. All of our lives we have been programmed to accept the word of authorities. It started with our parents, other adults, teachers, and governmental authorities, and it moves to anyone that we perceive has authority to tell us what to do. Authority is why we tend to believe experts.

Liking

If you've ever really liked someone, you know how hard it can be to turn them down. That's why Tupperware has your friends throw Tupperware parties for you. People are much more likely to buy if they like the person selling an item.

Scarcity

If you can't seem to get something then it must be more valuable. Think about the latest game or toy at Christmastime. That's why we have "limited-time" offers or "only limited quantities available" in our sales copy.

Affiliate Showcase Case Study

So how does all of this play into a successful launch? Let's take a look at the launch of Affiliate Showcase, a site that went from zero to a half-million-dollars' worth of sales in a six-month period.

Imagine you're sitting in your basement. Your desk is a large folding table, and you sit staring into a blank computer screen with your mind going wild with the possibilities. For months, you have worked on building a system that you think will solve a real problem and enable thousands of people to earn a decent living, and still have the freedom of working out of their own homes just as you do.

Your persistence has paid off, and you've managed to convince one of the most decent and respected leaders in the industry to help you design and promote your new system. You've tested the system and it works. Now the time has come to let other people into the system. You're hopeful it will go well, but scared to death that it will be a flop.

The first step is to invite in a couple hundred "beta" testers. Jim Daniels, your co-creator of the new Affiliate Showcase system, is a very likeable person. He already has the respect of thousands of people who have become his subscribers and customers. Within the industry, Jim is an authority on making a living on the Internet and the author of a book on the subject that automatically positions him as an expert. Jim is a likeable, respected authority who is telling people they should become testers. According to Cialdini, likeability and authority are good tools to use when you want to influence the masses.

In the invitation, you tell people there are only a few beta positions available and those positions will fill rapidly. Now the scarcity factor is kicking in, and you are implying that many other people will be taking advantage of the offer. That gives you implied social proof.

The offer is something that is exclusive to only 200 individuals, and you are giving them the opportunity to be one of a very select group with immediate access to something that other people will have to wait some time for. People feel special for being included in this select group and grateful that you are choosing them out of the thousands of available people.

There is one more twist to the invitation that you don't immediately think will encourage participation. In the invitation, you tell them that, even though this product is in "beta," and there might be numerous problems at the start, they still have to pay the full monthly fee to be a "beta" member. In effect, you are requiring them to pay you money to test your software. Why ask them to pay you—aside from the money?

The truth is that people don't value what they don't pay for. How many free e-books have you downloaded to your hard drive and never spent the time to read? By paying you for the service, the service immediately becomes more valuable to your members because they personally invested in it. If you are paying a monthly fee for a service, you are much more likely to make use of it. You are also more likely to pay attention and to get real value out of it.

The first 200 sign-ups go really well, and so you invite 2,000 more. Social proof is really starting to click in. People can see more visitors pouring into the site and know they are in an exciting group. The second wave is moving as if it's clockwork, and that is when the nightmare starts.

Jim goes into his e-mail service and, instead of selecting 2,000 more people to invite, he accidentally unselects 2,000, which sends the offer out to another 158,000 people instead of the 2,000 he was going to send to—and all of them are dying to get into the beta program.

The site is completely overwhelmed with the traffic, taking 15 minutes to load, and you are worried. While you scramble to fix technical issues, you communicate with your members: "Yes, we are aware of the problems and working to fix them." "Yes, we will let you know the second that we are ready to launch." And most importantly, "NO, don't tell *anyone* about the site." The last thing you want is for more people to come in and slow your system even more.

The pressure cooker starts heating up. Have you ever told someone a secret and asked him or her not to tell anyone? Okay. Let me put it this way: Have you ever told tens of thousands of people a secret and told them not to tell anyone? You can imagine the result.

To make it even more interesting, the beta testers are watching each other closely to make sure that no one breaks the rules. You pile on the pressure by telling your beta testers that if anyone tells anyone about the site you will personally kick him or her out of the system and never allow him or her to return. Then, the finger-pointing starts. Back and forth, people are accusing each other of letting the word out, and others are vehemently denying that they are the ones doing it. Then you track down a couple of offenders and kick them out of the system as promised.

You can imagine the pressure building. People make huge plans to tell other people about the site when it launches; rumors are flying everywhere. The launch is an event that has taken on a life bigger than the product itself. The launch is a huge success. In the course of six months, you bring in a quarter-million dollars, which at the time is decent money. That's the power of a successful launch.

So how do you make it happen for you? To create massive results, you need to do a number of things within a concentrated time frame. Here are just a few things that you need to build in order to create a successful launch:

- Launch team
- Partners
- Demand
- Credibility
- Social proof
- Authority
- Anticipation
- Proof
- Scarcity

But 1st: Reality Check

However, before you can start even thinking about building any of those crucial items, you need to do a reality check:

- Is there any problem in the first place?
- Is it a big problem or just an annoyance?
- Do you have a solution for the problem?
- Is there a demand for your solution?
- Is the need for your solution immediate?
- Is there already a solution out there?
- Is your solution affordable and cost-effective?
- Can you deliver your solution in time to meet the need?
- Is your solution easy?
- Is your solution simple?
- Is your solution easy to explain?
- Is your solution the best available?
- Will other people be willing to spread the word about what you have to offer?
- Will the culture allow your solution?
- Does your solution cause other problems?
- Will you offend people with your solution?
- Have people tried your solution before?
- Can you prove that your solution works?
- Will people recommend your solution?
- Is there at least one existing community that has the problem?
- Does the community have key influencers?
- Can you produce the solution at a profit?
- Can you support the solution?
- Does the solution create a legal liability for you?
- Does the solution meet your moral standards?
- Does the launch move you towards your primary goals in life?
- Can you measure the effects of your solution?
- Do other people see the value of your solution?

There are, of course, endless questions that you can ask that will help you determine whether your ideas are valid, valuable, and moving you towards your goals. At some point, you will make the choice to proceed or not to proceed, but before you make that final decision to move forward, make sure that you have asked enough questions to know whether you are being realistic.

You don't always have to be realistic. You can choose to move forward on a project despite knowing that the odds are not in your favor. People have created countless wonders when their plans were not realistic. However, there can be a very real cost to pay for ignoring reality. You should always be aware of exactly what risks you are taking when you make the choice.

Goals

Once you have done your reality check, you are ready to define your launch goals. We talked about setting your goals for your life, and launch goals are just as crucial. You may be trying to drive sales or prospects, or build your reputation. Whatever you are trying to do, you need to put your goals in measurable terms.

Insight Rendition

There are many ways to deliver the same message, and the method or methods to render those insights are crucial to the launch process. That means that you should decide as early as possible how you are going to deliver your solution.

If you are delivering information, knowledge, skills, or even your own reflections on your experiences, you can deliver that information in dozens of formats. See the chart on page 169 that lists a few of them to get your thinking started.

One of the big choices is whether your delivery method is electronic, physical, or in person. All of the methods are available to you. All have their advantages and disadvantages. The important thing is to make the choice of methods you will be using early so that you can get the systems in place to deliver your solutions to your audience.

Newsletter articles

Blog postings

Magazine articles

Books

Software

E-books

Coaching

Speeches

Workshops

Seminars

Mentoring

Consulting

DVDs

CDs

Webcasts

Teleconferences

Streaming video feeds

Podcasts

Websites

PDF files

Printed newsletters

Postcards

Workbooks

Action plans

Screen capture videos

Networking

Joint ventures

Mailing lists

Direct mail

Telephone calls

Television

Radio

Billboards

Display advertising

Press releases

E-mails

Non-profit organizations

Corporate training

Focus groups

Research results

Point-of-sale advertising

Trade shows

Concerts and events

Community organizations

Naming

Now is the time to start thinking about what you are going to call your solution. Here are some things to consider:

- What would your customers like you to call it?
- Is the name easy to say?
- Can people spell it?
- Is there more than one way to spell it?
- Is it too long?
- Does it convey a benefit?
- Will it offend anyone?
- Is it distinctive?
- Does it match your solution?
- What kind of a name do you want?
- Can you trademark it?
- Does it have a twist to it?
- Does it rhyme?
- Does it use alliteration?
- Can people repeat it?
- Can people remember it?
- Does it describe what you do?
- Does it include your name?
- Does the name include numbers or symbols?
- Does the name include abbreviations?
- Does the name include a place name?
- Does the name have two or more meanings?
- Does the name have religious, sexual, or political implications?
- What associations will the name evoke?
- Will the name appear in print?
- Is a domain name with the name available?

Copywriting

Copywriting is the art of using words to sell, and a copywriter is the person that writes those words. Are you a good copywriter who wants to take the time to write your own copy, or would you like to have someone else write it for you? Either way, you need solid copywriting throughout the launch process. I've had quite a bit of experience both ways, and I wish I could tell you that I've found the perfect solution. I can tell you what the answer is. I just can't make it easy for you.

The answer is to have the perfect person doing your copywriting. Finding that person is a little tougher. Whether you ultimately decide to have someone write the copy for you or not, I suggest that you do a first draft yourself. You need to know what the process is. You also need to be aware of the points that you want your sales copy to make.

As long as you have to take the time to go through the process in your mind, you might as well spend the time to write the first draft of the sales letter. If you decide to bring in a professional, at least he or she will have a starting point to work with, and who knows? You may like your efforts. You can always have a professional tweak your work, and it will probably cost you a little less if he or she doesn't have to do the heavy lifting.

Here are some key questions that you may want to think about when considering professionals:

- What is their experience level?
- Have they been successful?
- Does their style match your solution?
- What do their customers say about them?
- Are they professional?
- Do they offer ongoing support?
- Will they rewrite materials at no charge if you don't like the results?
- Do they offer a written contract?
- Do they return your calls?
- Is it cost-effective to outsource your copywriting to this person?
- Have they written copy for your niche?

- Have you looked at samples of their work?
- Can they write your copy in time?
- What kind of guarantees do they offer?

Great copywriters aren't inexpensive, and you should be aware that you can lose thousands of dollars by making the wrong choice. Take the time to know the copywriter you are dealing with and start by testing out your relationship one step at a time. You may want to consider a small test project to see how you work together and whether or not the person can produce the type of results that you are looking for. Great copywriting makes a huge difference in your bottom-line launch results. Copywriting can take you to the top or keep you on the bottom, so make the best choices that you can.

Scarcity Tactics

Imagine that you are shopping for a new car. You've identified the make and model that you want and have been price shopping for weeks. Tired and frustrated, you walk into the local dealer's show-room and look around at the models on the floor. Unfortunately, there are no cars with the metallic blue finish that you like so much. Head down, you ask the salesperson if there are any cars that have the paint finish you want. The salesperson quickly returns. There is one car available if you grab it now, but it's a very popular color and they can't promise that it will be there tomorrow. How much room do you have for negotiation?

The lower the number available, the more people want them. People don't realize how much they want something until they can't get it. That means that taking things away makes things more valuable. You can take things away by:

- ☐ Specifying the amount of time something is available.
- ☐ Reducing the number that they can purchase.
- ☐ Removing some of the materials they receive when they buy a package.

Remember: People naturally procrastinate. If you give them the opportunity to wait, they will. Creating scarcity helps to do away with procrastination. That means that you should restrict not only your product or service, but the availability of the offer itself to make it a limited-time offering or a quantity-limited offer. But, the real key to fine-tuning your offers is justifying your restrictions. If people don't believe you, scarcity will seem to be a deceptive tactic and nothing more.

At all costs, stay away from those scripts that change the deadline daily. People aren't dumb. But, there are often very real reasons for restricting an offer. A coach, for example, only has so much time and can only take on a certain number of clients. Of course, you can reopen your program when more slots become available, but, if you are going to close a program at a certain number of clients, then you need to do exactly what you say you are going to do.

You can also take away other parts of the offer in a particular time frame. Here are a few things you can take away if they procrastinate:

- ☐ Sections of your package
- ☐ Bonuses
- ☐ Premium packaging
- ☐ Coaching
- ☐ Free support
- ☐ Free shipping
- ☐ Teleconference and Webcasts
- ☐ Memberships
- ☐ Consulting

Make sure you are believable. You never want people to feel that the scarcity is a manipulative ploy. Make sure that you always provide a reason for what you are doing.

Timing

Now you need to decide when you want to launch. This is where many people seem to get into trouble. Typically, people try to develop a product and launch it at the same time. Unless you have many people to help, I'd encourage you to first set a target date, next develop your product, and then, after you have completed the product, set the actual launch date.

No, that doesn't mean that you can't start building prospects long before your product is completed. In fact, I encourage you to do exactly that. You don't want to base your launch date on a production schedule that may or may not be met. Optimally, you will know that your product is solid and that sales and promotion systems, including any Website or shopping cart system, are in place at least four weeks before your projected launch date. If you don't have at least that much time, you will be missing out on potential sales.

You need to consider when your competitors are doing their own events. You may want to schedule yours to avoid conflicts and a divided audience. When I launched the *Info Product Blueprint* DVD, CD, and workbook package, I planned my release date months in advance, but, once I set my date, I discovered that another huge product release was happening on the same day. I didn't want to compete directly with another offer that many of my joint venture partners were taking part in, so I pushed back my announcement to avoid the conflict.

Unfortunately, the other launch kept delaying their release date, too. Eventually, more than 30 product releases were waiting on this one huge event. When that day finally came, everyone had been waiting for more than a month to tell the public about their products and the week that *Info Product Blueprint* launched more than 30 other new products appeared in the same niche. That type of a pile-up doesn't help anyone's bottom line. Look at what is going on in your niche, and find the optimal time to avoid pockets of noise.

Typically, launches follow seasonal trends. In the Internet marketing product arena, the busy times are traditionally from September through November and then late January through June. Because it isn't a retail industry, the holidays and summers are slow. Retail stores are the opposite. Whatever your market trends are, you may want to consider launching in quieter periods to avoid clutter. If you can't get your message out because of other promotions, it won't help you to be in a busy time period—even if that is when your customers are looking.

Building buzz and generating prospects takes time, so don't short-change the amount of time that you have to get it right. Consider the fact that your potential promotional partners have schedules of their own and that you want to give them plenty of notice so they can get your launch on their calendar. Also, don't forget your family. Any launch will not only mean increased time and stress on you, but also on your loved ones.

Setting Your Budget

It's important to know what your budget is before you start committing resources. Your available budget may have a huge impact on how you deliver your solution, the timing for your launch, and how you implement your promotional plan. It's amazing how much you can do with little money, but funding makes the world a heck of a lot easier, and there's no doubt that a little money wisely spent can make a huge difference in the amount of impact that you create.

Go through all of the areas that you are going to need to support and start adding up the projected costs. Then start comparing options. Here are some choices that can really make a difference in your budget:

- Paid advertising or PR campaign.
- Physical product or digital delivery.
- Paid copywriter or write your own copy.
- Huge physical package or single CD.
- Professional studio or on-location video.
- Professional voiceover talent or speaking yourself.
- Custom music or licensed music.
- Custom graphics or stock graphics.
- Database-driven Website or brochure-style Website.
- Contest-driven promotion or no contest promotion.
- Audio or video.
- Live events or Webcasts.
- Traditional publisher or self-published.
- Live support or automated help desk.
- Holding your own event or speaking at others.

- Flash Website or HTML Website.
- Custom programming or open-source software.
- Monthly services or one-time purchases.

Setting Your Pricing

The first thing that you need to know about pricing your products and services is that product pricing is hard. Most people assume that you want to find the perfect price where you can maximize the profits immediately. That may not be the case at all. Your goal may be to achieve more visibility as the leading expert in your field or to establish the value of future product offerings. In either of those cases, generating the maximum immediate profit may be a secondary issue.

Pricing and positioning go together. We know that the price of a product or service affects the number of sales, but what we can't always tell is whether raising the price will cause sales to go up or down. If you are offering a 14-day vacation to Hawaii that covers all airfare, hotel, food, and entertainment costs for only $99, then you may raise some suspicions about the legitimacy of your offer. On the other hand, you may be able to sell an e-book for $997, but you will definitely limit the number of takers by setting that price.

When I created the *Info Product Blueprint* package, I asked several industry experts what the price should be. The answers ranged from a low of $395 to a high of $4,997. That's a pretty wide range for a product.

Let's say you have the ability to see the future and could accurately predict what sales would be at either price point. If you only sell 100 copies at $4,997, you will have total sales of $499,700. On the other hand, if you sell 20 times as many copies at the lower price, you will have sales of $790,000.

Is that better? It might be. You would have 2,000 customers instead of 100 customers, and you'd have more money. That sounds better, but it might not be in the long term. You might be trying to position yourself as a person who sells products and services that are worth thousands of dollars. Maybe you want to serve a select group of customers that will be willing to purchase high-ticket products.

You certainly want to consider the lifetime value of those customers. It can be much more difficult to service 2,000 customers. If your product is personal coaching, then trying to mentor 2,000 clients individually might be a nightmare. Think about whether you are looking for exposure and credibility, or pure profits. You may be able to get both, but before you start, you want to know which one is more important to you if you have to make crucial choices later. If you want to have hundreds of thousands of people reading what you have to say, don't offer them a $997 e-book.

To position your solution correctly, you need to know what your competitors are offering and who they are. How is your product different from theirs? What are their prices? What price range reflects what you want people to think about your product?

You also need to consider your expenses. You can scale digitally delivered products very effectively without raising your expenses, but the number of sales affects all projects to some degree. You definitely need to consider customer support costs, the costs of promoting and selling the products, and the costs of your overhead that may grow with the number of people that you reach.

Sometimes, pricing should be set by answering the question: "How much is this worth to my customer?" However, sometimes the better question is: "How much will my customer be losing if they don't purchase my product?" Just make sure that you aren't selling at a price that you can't maintain and support over the long haul, or leaving money on the table that your audience is more than willing to give you.

You also need to consider products that you could offer in connection with your main offering. You may want to ask yourself the following questions:

- Will you have an upsell?
- Are you offering a lower-priced version?
- Are you offering back-end products or services?
- Are you bundling additional products?
- Are you charging for support?
- How much are your charging for shipping and handling?

You may be offering volume discounts, tiered pricing, multiple payment options, or recurring billing options. You may also want to consider whether your pricing is too complex. The confused prospect never buys, so offering complex options will often lower your conversion rates (your sales).

Some other questions to consider include:

- Is this a sale price?
- Is it a loss leader? (designed to attract leads instead of sales)
- Do you want to offer additional rights to your products? (private label or resale rights)
- Is this solution something that people purchase on a regular basis?

Back-End Products

Once you have an initial sale, you have a much greater chance of selling more products and services to the same customer. You've already gotten their attention, identified their willingness to purchase your products, started to build that all important relationship, and overcome their initial objections. Now is the perfect time to start thinking about back-end products and services.

You can offer additional information on the same topic, offer the same information in a different format, offer products from other vendors, encourage them to join a membership site, or attend a live event.

Creating Your Action Plan

By this stage, you should be starting to create your own personal action plan. You can start as simply as sketching out a flow chart of what you want to do on a piece of paper. Don't worry; we have an entire chapter coming up that will tell you exactly how to start building your systems.

Product Creation

Any products and services developed for your launch need to be finished well in advance of the actual launch date. I hope that you know clearly what your audience is looking for and what audience members want you to provide them. Now all you need to do is make sure that you get their problems solved and create a quality, tested product in a professional package in time to make sure that you can reach the maximum number of eager prospects. I wish that I could say that it always happens, but in truth it almost never does. Most people are natural-born procrastinators, and I'm no exception. What I can tell you is that, the more that you have done well in advance, the better off you are.

If you are selling a physical product, such as a CD set, you need to make sure the fulfillment process is completely in place long before you actually have to deliver a product. At this point, you can decide whether you want to create your product yourself, hire someone to create it for you, or find existing materials that you can use for a product.

Product creation is a book in itself. The whole idea around the creation of *Info Product Blueprint* was to give people the comprehensive information that they need to create information products. For now, just remember that you don't have to do it all by yourself. Before you launch, review where I talk about team building and product creation in this book and make sure to grab additional resources at *TheImpactFactor.com/ resources/*.

Before the product development stage, be sure to check out the comprehensive information on developing products, which is available at *InfoProductBlueprint.com.*

Website Development

Your Website is your prospect capture system, your salesperson, your customer support platform, your positioning statement, and a reflection of all that you stand for. Whether you decide to design, create, and maintain it yourself or put it in the hands of a seasoned professional, you will need to be deeply involved in making sure that it represents you in the best possible way, converts your prospects into evangelists for your ideas, and supports them in the way that your audience deserves.

Even if you are outsourcing your Website development, you need to clearly define the goals for your Website in advance, create a general layout and a flow chart for the way that you want your audience to move through the processes, and imagine how your site should look on the screen. Your site should be simple to navigate and should automatically move your prospects directly to a clear call to action. Colors and images can be important, but should not distract your prospects from taking action. The content should not overwhelm. It should enlighten.

Payment Processors

If you want to collect money, you have to process payments. That almost certainly means that you need the ability to process credit cards, and credit cards can be a nightmare.

Think of credit card payments the same way you think of cars and computers: They are wonderful when they work correctly and awful when they don't. If you aren't careful, you can be out thousands of dollars due to processing problems, refunds, chargebacks and hidden fees. That doesn't even mention the fact that merchant accounts are completely skewed to the banks, which means that they often have the ability to take your money and hang onto it for long periods of time, which may make it impossible for you to meet your own financial requirements. It's wonderful when money comes pouring into your checking account automatically while you sleep, but it's another thing entirely to have it disappear when you least expect it.

You definitely want multiple options for your customers to complete their payments. Most people want to pay via credit card, but many would prefer to make payments through PayPal, check, or even telephone billing. Luckily, you can give your customers all of these options online.

Setting up a merchant account for processing credit cards takes time. If you already have a merchant account for a retail business, you may want to check and see if they are willing to process Internet credit card payments. Your local bank may be willing to set up a merchant account for you, but many do not. For most local banks, the Internet is a very scary place full of scams and potential for fraud.

Preferably, deal with a merchant account provider that is familiar with online payment processing. There are resources for merchant accounts on the resources page at *TheImpactFactor.com/resources/*.

Be sure to think big when you start talking about how much income you expect to receive. Merchant account providers may freeze your own funds if they start seeing unexpected levels of sales coming through your account, and you may not need a merchant account at all. Many services will handle everything for you for a straight percentage fee. Options include:

- **PayPal.**

   This widely used service has gotten a lot of exposure because eBay purchased the company and is using it as a preferred payment system. PayPal doesn't cost anything to join.

- **ClickBank.**

  This program works well for digital products and has a built-in affiliate system.

- **2Checkout.**

  This is another low-cost option.

Here are some other factors to consider:

- Credit review may increase the amount of time required to obtain a merchant account.

- Carefully review all of the terms of the merchant account agreement.

- Make sure that the company will give you a high enough credit limit.

- Not all shopping cart systems work with all processors.

- Establish the lines of communication with your processor early.

- Notify them of any anticipated changes in sales volume.

- Test your system completely before launch day.

- Check the accuracy of updates between your merchant account and your shopping cart system.

Fulfillment and Delivery

If you are delivering your product or service digitally, it will be easier and less expensive than a physical product. One clear advantage of digital products is that your delivery costs typically don't rise proportionally to the number of copies that you sell.

That doesn't mean that things will necessarily be problem-free. Here are a few things to double-check:

- Make sure that your Website delivers the product quickly, clearly, and consistently every time that someone orders.

- Make sure that people who are new to the Internet can clearly understand how to receive their product.

- Be sure to tell people what to do if there are problems.

If you are shipping a physical product, it gets even more involved. Choosing a fulfillment company is a crucial factor in your success. Here are some things that a quality fulfillment company can do for you:

- Printing
- Product duplication
- Order-taking
- Graphics
- Packaging
- Shipping
- Returns
- Customer service

Other considerations when selecting a fulfillment company include:

- What their current customers think of them
- Their current financial situation
- The niches that they currently service regularly
- The quality of the products that they produce
- Their level of service
- The volume of output that they can quickly produce
- Up-front and set-up costs
- Costs per unit
- Support costs
- Shipping policies and options
- Turnaround time on custom work
- Whether they outsource some services
- Current and planned equipment levels
- Formats and types of media available
- Artwork requirements
- Return policies
- Shipping policies

Make sure that you check the fulfillment house out completely before committing fully to a long-term relationship.

Here are a few things to avoid:

- Last-second orders
- Unknown shipping costs
- Countries known for high levels of fraud
- Ordering without an estimate
- Sending your only copy to the fulfillment house
- Not setting up shipping and refund policies in advance
- Not asking for a delivery signature
- Not including "getting started" instructions in the package
- Not including support information in the package
- Not collecting full contact and shipping information
- Not tracking shipments

Testimonials

Testimonials are a great way to give your potential customers the confidence to know that they are working with someone that they can trust. If you haven't gathered some great testimonials, you need to do it now. Unless you are a Fortune 500 company, first-time visitors have no way of knowing how well you will respond to their needs.

I can tell you my service is great and that my customers love my products and services, but coming from me most anything that I say will come off as arrogance. In order to be effective, you need to design your testimonials. Here's an example of a poor testimonial:

"I love your product!"

—Anonymous

What's wrong with loving your product? Nothing! But notice that it doesn't really tell your audience why your product is so great, and it doesn't tell them who thinks it's great, either! In order to be effective, testimonials need to be specific, and prospects need to have the confidence that a real person made the comments and believes what they said.

How about this example?

> *"I am an amateur artist who recently ordered your Artist's Best easel. I just had to write and let you know how satisfied I am with your product! The wood, finish, and craftsmanship on my easel were superb. It was shipped sooner than I expected and putting it together was not really difficult.*
>
> *"I honestly thought that I would never be able to afford my own easel. It is always a little scary ordering over the Internet from companies that are not known to you, but I am so glad that I took a chance on you!"*

—Jackie Conte, Vero Beach, FL

This person is only "satisfied," but, notice how much more personal this testimonial is. The customer talks about the fears we all have and the way it worked out for her.

The good news is that, if you know how to do it, getting quality testimonials isn't anywhere near as hard as most would think. The hidden secret—that somehow seems to elude most people when getting testimonials—is very simple. All you need to do is ask for them.

Send existing customers an e-mail and let them know that their opinions are important to you. Ask them to give specific examples of ways that you have helped them. Here's a sample e-mail for generating some testimonials:

> *"Just a quick note to ask your help. We are currently looking for some great 'specific' testimonials to put up on our various Websites from people like yourself.*
>
> *"It would be great if you could take just a second to hit the reply button and type in a few lines to tell us about something that I've been able to do for you that was helpful or something that you like about our products and services we could share with the visitors to our Websites.*

> *"If you are willing to share your experience with us, we will post the best ones to our Websites along with a link to your Website. Hopefully, that will generate extra traffic to your site and help us give our people the confidence that they need to become part of our family."*

Here's an added bonus. You may get a pile of wonderful comments that make your day!

Video testimonials are probably the toughest testimonials to get, but they are the best format to leverage. You can use a video testimonial in a DVD or stream it on a Website, you can strip out the audio and use it in a podcast or audio download, and you can transcribe the words and use them in text format on your Website or in print format in printed materials.

Partners

The good thing is that you don't have to do this all by yourself. In fact, if you are determined to do everything yourself, you are severely limiting the amount of impact that you can create. Partners can help you in all facets of your launch. Here are just a few areas to get you thinking:

- Introductions
- Pricing
- Creation
- Testimonials
- Promotion

You've seen from the example of Jim Daniels the effect that a single joint venture partner can have on bottom-line results. Now imagine the effect that a couple hundred joint venture partners can have.

If you have identified the key influencers within your target networks, the next step is to build real relationships and motivate them to spread the word about what you are doing.

Here's something that I want you to remember: I'm just as guilty about forgetting it as everyone else is, so let's agree to keep reminding each other about this fact.

Partners are people. They wake up and they have fears, hopes, and dreams. They worry, plan, and set goals. They have a life with family, friends, and customers. They have problems, successes, and challenges every day. It's obvious, but it should always be the first thing that we think about when we start to build a relationship. Put yourself in the key influencer's shoes for just a second.

You are busy—excessively busy most likely. Each day you wake up and thousands of people want your attention. Your family wants more time with you. Your kids are growing up quickly, and your spouse feels that he or she is the low person on your priority list.

Because you are a key influencer, not only do people think they need your time, they really do need your time. You have something unique to offer they can't get any other place. Maybe it's your skills, your knowledge, your experience, or just your particular take on life. Whatever it is, it's what a large number of people need.

You really want to help. It's not just an act with you. It's the reason that you started doing this in the first place. You love the fact that people are finding value in what you are doing, and you want to share everything that you can offer with as many people as possible in the time that you have.

And that's where the rub comes in. There is only so much of you to offer. Your family wants time, your community wants time, your customers want time, and that's just the start of the list. Now everyone who sees how you influence people wants time.

Most of the people that are contacting you are saying the same things. They just want a little bit of your time, and they can give you a ton of money. The volume of these requests is building. Each day you receive more than 1,000 e-mails, and you feel compelled to respond. After all, these people are responding to your message, and you want to give back. If you spend two minutes on each e-mail, you would spend 33 hours answering e-mails each day.

You try to automate. You try to focus. You also try to be careful, because these people can burn you. Last week you promoted a new system only to find out that the person who created it took your customer's money and ran. It looked professional, it had all of the value, and you thought that it would be great for the people that you influence, but personal problems got in the way. The person who created it was going through a divorce and just disappeared. Now people who trusted you are left holding the bag and looking to you to make it right.

So now, you are wary. You start limiting the people that you recommend. You have a responsibility to the people who look to you for advice. Besides, you have bills to pay yourself. Those kids aren't going to get to college if you don't keep putting food on the table. So you spend most of your time trying to figure out how you can serve your growing list of prospects, meet your own goals in life, and still put food on the table.

Don't get me wrong. You love seeing people. There are many wonderful, exciting people, and you love to spend time with them. That's one of the joys of getting out of the house and speaking at live events. You get to share your experiences with a group of people who need what you have to offer, make a few friends, and see what's going on in the rest of the world.

Of course, there is always the person who comes up to you and immediately starts pitching his or her latest idea, but you understand. You've done it yourself a time or too. They will quickly learn that it doesn't get them too far.

You are aware of the people around you. Some of the people are such a joy. You notice them spending time with some of the less-well-known people at the event. They offer their seat to an older person who has been standing in the back. They smile, laugh, and seem relaxed among some of the more frantic attendees.

You don't hear them constantly mentioning what their next project is, and you are curious, so you make it a point to ask them. They quickly and clearly tell you about their next project, and ask you how their project can benefit you. Clearly, they want to help you meet your own goals. You stop and think. Your creative mind is exploring all of the possibilities. There is always a way to leverage any asset. Later that night your mind is still going.

A month passes, and you've moved on to new projects. You check your orders for the day and notice a name on an order form. Your new friend has purchased your product. Then you notice that they have also signed up for your affiliate program—that's another sale in my pocket and—who knows—maybe they will promote it.

The next day, you get a message on your voice mail system. Your new friend wants to interview you on a Webcast and promote your product. He only has a small list, but he's eager to find out exactly what he can do to maximize your sales.

You do the interview, and your friend really showcases what you have to offer. He sells a couple copies of your product and posts the interview on his Website, where it attracts a few more sales over the coming weeks. For your next big launch, he follows your instructions exactly and starts to produce some results for you. This person is amazing. He actually follows through. You get the picture. Who gets your attention when they come looking for a partner for their project?

By now, you are getting the impression that all of this relationship stuff takes time. It does take time, so start now. Does that mean that you have to be best friends with everyone that promotes for you? Absolutely not, but if you are you will get better results.

So let's say that you've been building real relationships with top-level people for ages. You've bought their products, promoted them, helped them with their launches, met them at live events such as jvAlert, given them samples of your work, know their personal interests, and convinced them that you are completely professional, dependable, and trustworthy. Now it's time to start building for your launch, so what should you be doing right now?

Now you need to think about options. The typical "event"-based launch requires partners to commit to a specific timeframe. The whole point of an "event" is that it concentrates all of the attention of a particular market on you for a clearly defined period. That may make it difficult for certain potential partners to participate. Maybe they are planning on launching their own products in your time frame or maybe they would just like to go on vacation.

To ensure that you have the maximum participation levels, you need to make sure that you clearly set your launch date as early as possible. Early notice allows partners to include your launch on their schedules before those schedules are full. It always allows you to stake a claim on the particular time frame. Your competitors will be less likely to put their own launches in your time frame if they know what to avoid.

Your partners need to know what benefits they will receive from participating in your launch. Don't forget to think outside of the box. Partners are interested in their commissions, but they are also interested in how promoting your product makes them appear in the eyes of the people that they influence.

Here are some key motivating factors to keep in mind:

- Deliver a quality product.
- Give great value to their audience.
- Communicate with partners early.
- Make it easy for partners to participate.
- Give them all of the materials that they need.
- Give them access to your product.
- Use social proof to encourage participation.
- Appeal to their competitive spirit.
- Build the excitement.
- Use scarcity.
- Report results quickly.
- Offer to customize promotions for them.
- Deliver quality customer service.

Your sales page for your partners is every bit as important as your sales page for your customers, so don't make it a rush job. Spell out the key benefits and the key responsibilities. You should clearly let partners know you expect them to do certain things, and you should try to hold them to it. Most partners know that they should invest heavily in promoting your launch in order to get the best results, but most of them will procrastinate, forget, get busy, and do nothing—the same as the rest of us—if they aren't held responsible. You need to be the one to follow up.

Use social proof to encourage partners to sign up immediately. Once you land your first high-profile partner, you can use that person to encourage other top-level people to promote your project. Always ask partners who they might know that would be interested in being part of your team of partners. By the way, start thinking of your partners as a team. After all, you are all working together to succeed.

At times, you may want to limit the number of partners to make it more attractive for top-level partners to participate. After all, top-level partners don't want to be just one of hundreds of people sending out e-mails on launch day. They want to be unique. At other times, you may want to have as many partners and affiliates as possible. Is this a high-ticket, low-volume launch, or a low-price, high-volume launch? Pricing may affect the number and type of partners you want to attract.

Not all partner lists are equal. Some partners may have hundreds of thousands of subscribers; others only have hundreds. That does not mean that the large lists will necessarily perform better for your launch. Often, small, targeted, and well-maintained lists will do significantly better than larger, older lists that partners have neglected. Lists that are out of your immediate niche may not produce results as high as more targeted lists. However, in saturated markets it's often good to broaden your reach when you are searching for new prospects.

Invest the time to give partners quality promotional aids and sample copy. Experienced marketers will not use the copy verbatim, but it makes it much easier for them to have the key benefits to work with. The more innovative you can be, the more your promotions will stand out. Cover all types of media to broaden your impact.

Partners can't effectively market anything if they don't have the product. If your product is expensive to produce, you may need to select key partners to receive the full package, but you can usually give access to most materials in digital format so that all partners can have a firsthand look at what they are recommending. If you can afford it, make sure that you get physical copies to all key partners.

Set up a partner-only blog to update partners on the progress of your launch. As new partners become involved, let the group know exactly what is going on and what to expect. Make sure that you have an autoresponder series in place so that all partners get the initial information when they sign up, but use the blog for all updates to avoid problems and confusion when sending out updates. If you send out a bad link in an e-mail, then it goes out to everyone. If you send a notice of a blog post to everyone and discover that it is a bad link, you can fix it immediately.

Partners can be similar to little kids: They crave attention, are competitive, and love toys. You can effectively leverage these facts by creating a contest with innovative incentives for your top partners. Reporting results to your partners as your launch progresses builds the excitement, and many partners have found themselves doing many more promotions than they originally planned, in order to hold onto a top spot or to claim a prize that they just had to have. Try to come up with innovative incentives. Most of your top partners may be able to buy almost anything they want, but new is always interesting, and articles that are scarce or contribute to building their own business can be powerful motivators.

Keep your partners informed and notify them quickly when they make sales. A sale is a wonderful motivator for many people. Also be sure to follow up quickly with any problems that your partners or their customers may have. If you keep your partner's customers happy, your partners will be even happier.

Affiliate Systems

If you are going to pay joint venture partners and affiliates for referring people to your products and services, you need a system to track the sales that they refer and to calculate payments. Luckily, both joint venture partners and affiliates can use the same system.

Affiliate programs typically create a special, unique Web address called an affiliate link that the affiliate can refer people to when they are interested in your products and services. People who click on this link are tracked and, when they purchase a product, the system gives the person who referred them credit for the sale.

There are a wide range of features, functionality, and pricing, so it is difficult to know which options are best. The first decision that you need to make is whether to use an affiliate network, use a hosted shopping cart system, or purchase software and maintain your own in-house affiliate system.

Affiliate Networks

Affiliate networks have the advantage of already having a group of affiliates that may be interested in promoting your product. Affiliate Networks include the services ClickBank, PayDotCom, and ShareASale.

The good news is that you don't have to be a programmer to set up this type of system, and you get access to all of the potential partners. You don't have to worry about the software breaking down or, in some cases, even paying the affiliates. All you need to do is put your sales pages in the system and a simple piece of code on your Web page, and tell the system where your customers go to collect the product.

On the other hand, you are constrained by the limits of their system and their policies. You may have limited options to customize the program to meet your needs, and the affiliates may not service your particular market.

Shopping Cart Systems

Shopping cart systems allow people to select multiple items for sale until "checkout," when they process a single payment. Many eShopping cart systems have affiliate programs built in. Some shopping cart systems are limited in the number of features. Others may include such services as hosted e-mail. You do need to be aware that hosted shopping cart systems that offer e-mail services may experience e-mail delivery issues because anti-spam software and services may block delivery of e-mails coming from an entire server, even if you are not the person that is sending the spam.

Purchasing and Maintaining Affiliate Programs In-House

There are multiple shopping cart and affiliate program systems available for purchase and installation on your own servers. You need to realize that maintaining systems in-house can be very time-consuming and may require large amounts of expertise.

Autoresponder Systems

When marketing on the Internet, e-mail lists are crucial. To handle your e-mail lists, you need an autoresponder. I used to handle all of my e-mail lists with custom software on my own servers, but in today's atmosphere of e-mail filtering and blocking you should be using a quality outside service to make sure that your messages are getting through to as many people as possible.

With an autoresponder service, you can easily set up a simple form on your Website to allow people to sign up to receive e-mails from you. Autoresponder services typically allow you to easily send people a predefined set of messages on a schedule. You can also "broadcast" a message at any time to send a message instantly to everyone on your list.

You can use autoresponders to send out multiple-day e-courses, or allow your visitors to receive a special report or white paper instantly. You can also use autoresponders to mail newsletters, announcements, and updates to your list. Most services allow you to track the effectiveness of your messages at a glance using reports that track how many people open your messages and how many click on links within your message in real time. Anything you can put into an e-mail you can send using an autoresponder.

You can configure autoresponders to ask your customers to provide additional information, such as name, mailing address, or any other information that you would like to store. You do need to be aware that the more information you ask for, the less likely people will be to fill out your form and sign up.

For quality e-mail services, just refer to our resources page at *TheImpactFactor.com/resources/*.

List Building

Now that you have a way to handle your e-mails, you need to start collecting your audience. Please note that list building takes time and needs to be started early. Getting people to sign up for your e-mails can be very easy and rewarding. So let's explore a few methods for getting people on your list.

The first thing that you will probably want to consider is called an ethical bribe. Ethical bribes can be anything that you are willing to give someone to sign up for your list. In effect, you are bribing them to give you their name and e-mail address. Common examples of ethical brides include e-books, e-courses, videos, screen capture presentations, audio recordings, or even CDs and DVDs mailed directly to your prospects' house for the cost of shipping.

You can also use targeted advertising including "pay-per-click" advertising. You can conduct surveys and deliver the results to people who sign up for your list. You can joint venture with other list owners to refer subscribers between lists. You can write articles and submit them to online article directories and publications, requesting that they include a link to your newsletter signup form. If you are on a radio or television show, you can use those appearances to drive people to a signup form. Teleconferences and Webcasts can be great events that build your list. You can leave physical cards or promotional offers at physical stores. You can travel to events and give out information. You can speak in many different venues. You can reward others for sending you referrals. You can offer coaching or consultations. You can create assessment tools and provide reviews. The list goes on. There are many more ways to build a list included in our resources at *TheImpactFactor.com/resources/*.

The key fact is that you want to build your list in every way possible as early and quickly as possible.

So once you have your list, you need to build a real relationship with that list. The best way to do that is to take time. Repeatedly offer them value through your content and by rewarding them in any way that you can.

Moving the Free Line

Most people involved in marketing of any kind are familiar with the idea of the "sales funnel." A typical sales funnel will start by attracting prospects by offering free information and will move them by stages in to progressively higher and higher priced items. A sales funnel might include some of the following free items to try to attract a potential audience:

- Reports
- Videos
- Screen capture presentations
- Blogging
- Article marketing
- Newsletters
- Audio recordings
- E-books
- Press releases

As the prospects move through the sales funnel, you typically offer your audience products that increase in price. You may convince a prospect to purchase an e-book or a physical book in a bookstore as a low-priced product, sell them a home study course, and finally move them up into high-priced individualized coaching or live events.

I first heard the term *moving the free line* during a speaker presentation at a jvAlert Live event. Since that time, the concept has been widely discussed in Internet marketing circles. Marketers often offer low-cost, low-value resources at no cost to interest prospects, but the public is catching on to the fact that most of the resources are garbage. How many awful e-books have you downloaded that turned out to be nothing but worthless sales pitches?

As the public becomes more frustrated, that frustration creates an opportunity to profit from creating and giving away higher quality materials. Quality stands out in the crowd, because there are so many useless products. It's a relief to find a product that is really worth something. It's even better when you can get that information free.

"Moving the free line" is the idea that you should offer more valuable resources for free in order to let people know that what they are going to purchase is very valuable. It makes people think that, if you are giving away resources that are so valuable, your paid products must be even more valuable.

"Moving the free line" is extremely powerful because it heightens the perceived value of everything that you do. That makes it a hugely valuable tool for creating anticipation in a launch; however, you need to know that it's not a beginners technique. "Moving the free line" too soon can have devastating financial consequences, because what you are actually doing is putting off any monetization until the second or even optimally the third step of the process.

The questions that you need to ask yourself are:

1. Can I wait for the money?
2. Have I already built up a library of valuable materials that I can afford to give away?

Experienced marketers already have a stockpile of materials that they have produced and monetized, so it's easier for someone who has been building resources for a long time to give away some of them. After all, most likely, they have already generated income from those resources. In fact, they may just be sitting there unused. However, you may not have the time to wait. Whether you are moving ideas, products, or services, cash flow is a crucial element to your success, and, because cash flow is a product of time, you may not have much time, so you'd better be sure you have enough before you start giving things away.

Support

Making the sale is only half the battle. As soon as the sale is complete, your customers will start wondering whether they made the right decision. The ways that you address their concerns and reassure them that they have made the best possible choice can have a huge impact on your long-term success. Guaranteed, there will be problems. Here are a few things that you can do to avoid problems by giving great customer support:

- Set up a "help desk" system.
- Set up autoresponders to let people know that you have received their message.
- Answer e-mails quickly.
- Help them consume the product by clearly indentifying the next steps to take.
- Give them a printable copy of their invoice.
- Give them an unexpected bonus gift.
- Give them a follow-up phone call.
- Give them immediate access to as much of the product as possible online.
- Have support and return policies and procedures in place.
- Tell them how to use the product.
- Anticipate their questions and give them answers before they ask them.
- Give them additional resources.
- Train your support people.
- Include tracking information in follow-ups.
- Set up a user forum.

Congratulations! You've just created an amazing launch for your brilliant idea. You may be feeling a bit overwhelmed at this point, but don't worry. There are many things you do to increase your impact, but you don't have to do them all. There is an important rule to consider though.

Think of your launch as a checklist. Every item that I covered in this chapter is a line on the list with a big checkbox. Here's Ken's Checkbox Rule:

> "For every checkbox you check, you get exponential results."
>
> —Ken McArthur

So start checking! Don't worry; you will always have this book and the resources on our resource page at *TheImpactFactor.com/resources/* to help you through. Now let's build you a personal impact system to make it simple!

Live to See Your Success: Build a System

Almost every day, someone who is new will ask me where to start. They want that magic bullet to get them laser focused on success. Here's what I tell them:

- Find someone you trust who is doing what you want to do.

- Do what he or she does.

- Measure the results and compare to the results you want.

- Adjust your actions—in small ways—to see if the results improve.

- Repeat.

MTA Action System

In other words, take MTA Actions:

- Model.

- Test.

- Adjust.

Modeling successful people is the way to get amazing results in a short time, because successful people are different by definition. They are getting results that are not "normal." Their results are extraordinary. As my friend and mentor Glenn Dietzel says,

"Greater sameness will never get you better results." That means you want to model not what they are doing the same, but what they are doing differently.

Look at people who are trying to get a message to a mass audience. Most of them have a number of elements in common. For instance, they have:

- A Website
- Written materials
- A phone number

Maybe the top 3 percent have all of those things, plus they also have:

- A television show
- An outbound sales force
- Integrated advertising
- Direct mail

You want to take a good look at the things that are unique to the top 3 percent that the 97 percent don't have. Even more importantly, you want to look at what they are doing.

Automatic Reactions

Most of us do things automatically. You know it's true. Have you ever been driving only to come out of a daze and realize that you are halfway to a place that you never intended to go? Habits are powerful. We respond so automatically that in some cases it's almost impossible not to respond that way. It's built in.

Turkey mothers respond to the cheep-cheep sound of their chicks. In fact, they respond almost exclusively to that sound, and they do it automatically. Polecats are natural enemies of turkeys, and, when you place a stuffed polecat in a turkey pen, turkey mothers repeatedly and viciously attack the stuffed animal. But if you put a recorder inside the toy and play a recording of cheeping, the mothers will treat the stuffed animal just as though it were a chick. The response is automatic.

As humans, we do the same thing. What is your automatic response when you walk into a store and the salesperson asks, "May I help you?"

Most of us automatically say, "No, thanks. I'm just looking," but if the salesperson asks a different question, we may not have an automatic answer.

In fact, most top salespeople don't start by asking "May I help you?" and it makes a big difference in sales results. The top salespeople are doing something different. If you pay attention to what top people do differently, you can have significant success. That's why modeling is so powerful.

The MTA Action System is a very effective and simple system for getting quick results. "Model" what the top people do, "Test" the results, and "Adjust" for success. So, when I decided to build a massive impact system, I started by looking at what other successful people were doing. We all have 24 hours in a day, so how do people who are very successful manage to get results that others can't? What are they doing that other people aren't doing?

It Turns Out That They Build Systems.

Don't worry. Systems can be simple. After all, a system is just an organized set of objects and processes designed to accomplish a goal. Look at your body. You have a blood circulation system. It has objects (heart, arteries, blood, and so forth), it has processes (the heart pushes blood along a pre-determined path), and it has a goal (to spread oxygen and nutrients throughout the body). We all use systems every day. You have a system for getting ready for work, a system for checking your e-mail, and a system for keeping your teeth cavity-free. If we think about it at all, we realize that systems are a huge part of our lives. They can make our lives wonderful or miserable. I want your life to be wonderful, so let's talk about how to make that happen.

If Systems Are Common, What's so Different About the Top 3 Percent?

When I looked at the top 3 percent of people who were doing what I wanted to do, I found that all of the top 3 percent created powerful systems—and the other 97 percent didn't. Not only did the top people build powerful systems, but they think systematically about everything that they do. I decided to look at the systems they created so that I could take some MTA actions of my own.

Before I tell you what I found, let's travel back to the launch of Affiliate Showcase that I told you about earlier. Affiliate Showcase was one of my first big success stories. It started out with a bang, and, almost instantly, I had thousands of customers. That was instantly a problem because I was the only person in the world who knew anything about how Affiliate Showcase worked. I'd created it. I knew it inside out, but I hadn't really planned to succeed.

We all dream of success. We work hard to make it happen, but when it comes, it's always unexpected. One day I had no customers, and the next I had more than two thousand customers, and they all had questions that they wanted answered immediately. Imagine 2,000 anxious customers each with three or four urgent questions. Let's say that my new customers have 6,000 questions and it takes an average of 15 minutes to answer each question. That's 1,500 hours, which comes out to 37 weeks of work. Now imagine that they all want answers right now. That's not too far from the situation that I found myself in when Affiliate Showcase launched.

It turns out that there is an easier way. In some ways, life isn't nearly as complex as we often make it. In fact, if you select any 6,000 questions about Affiliate Showcase and put them into categories, you very quickly realize there are only about 20 basic questions that people ask. Sure, they may ask the question in slightly different ways, and they definitely don't all ask the same questions, at the same time, in the same order. But, when you start counting unique questions, there have only been about 20 distinct questions from hundreds of thousands of customers since April 2002. What I had was a natural place to create a system.

I would like to think you see the value of building a system when the very first idea pops into your head, but the truth is that sometimes we don't have a clue where to start. What if I'd tried to work out all of the potential problems for Affiliate Showcase before we launched? There is a very real danger that if you wait to build a system before you take other actions to create a business, you may never get started at all. That would be a real shame, so I'm going to suggest that you first take action and then build a system as you go.

In the case of Affiliate Showcase, the customer support issue came up long before we had a system in place to deal with customer support, so I took a little precious extra time to build the system as I handled customer support. Instead of quickly sending off an e-mail to a customer with a problem, I took the time to answer the entire question as completely as I possibly could. Not only did I answer the question, but I brought up related questions that they might have after they read my answers. I gave them extensive resources to give them more information not only on the topic they asked about, but also on related subjects.

It might take an hour or more to craft a carefully considered, detailed, and comprehensive response, but imagine the look on the customers' face when they got back that response. Then I stored off the comprehensive answer as a "standard response." Taking that time up front gave me quality material that I could use repeatedly. Once you fine-tune the response, it works as if it's clockwork.

Let's do the math again using a standard response. Twenty questions times one hour equals 20 hours. Much longer—and I have 5,980 questions to go! But, now copy and paste the appropriate answers into responses at one minute per question and you are suddenly down to 100 remaining hours. The total time invested is now 120 hours. That's down from 1,500 hours if I answered them all individually. That's the value of a system.

I've just described how I built a simple "low-tech" system. Now imagine that we automate that system with a "help desk" that has all 20 questions already in a Knowledge Base along with the answers. As a person asks a question, the system automatically searches for the answer, and, if it's there, it automatically delivers the answer and asks if the response has answered their question. If not, then it adds it to the database and a customer support representative fills out the answer in detail and adds it to the system.

So how do you take this simple example and apply it to your situation? Sure enough, there is a system to develop systems. Are you surprised? But before you can fully understand why systems are important, it is critical that you grasp the importance of systemic thinking.

What Is Systemic Thinking?

Systemic thinking is quite simply the ability to think about life in terms of systems. It is a mindset that can be learned and applied to business and to life. Systemic thinkers classify physical objects and their processes into systems. Some objects may be thought of as part of a larger system. Other objects may be decomposed into smaller and smaller objects.

A Brief Example of Systemic Thinking

You've just purchased a new car, and as you are waiting in the show-room for the salesperson to complete the paperwork, you notice a couple looking at your new car. As the proud new owner, you introduce yourself and tell John and Sally they are out of luck because you just signed the deal on the car. The three of you start discussing the pros and cons of your new car, and as you talk you notice something interesting about the couple. What you notice is that they think differently about the car. It's not their opinion of the car itself that's different. The actual way that they think is different.

To John, it's just a car—a hunk of metal with wheels that had better start when desired, and then reliably and safely transport him to his destination.

To Sally, it's part of a transportation system that includes roads, high-ways, bridges, traffic lights, signs, and millions of automobiles to move people and objects from one location to another.

The difference is that Sally sees everything as part of a system.

Sally's perspective seems a little odd, if you think about it. Most people don't think transportation system when they see a car. The majority—97 percent of people—see a car as a car. Sally seems to be the oddball. Actu-ally, she is the exception, and that means that she is exceptional. The top 3 percent are exceptions, too, because they are thinking about systems just as Sally is. That's the difference.

Once you start thinking about systems, you'll view the remainder of your life through a different pair of lenses that you will never lose. Once the light bulb goes on, you will understand and create systems that can produce amazing and powerful results by unlocking leverage, relationships, efficiencies, and ultimately enabling you to achieve the maximum impact that you seek in your lifetime and beyond.

So just how do you get started with systems? You've already started thinking about systems, so the next step is to...

Define Your Mission.

Let's talk about touchstones for a minute. A touchstone is a hard black stone, such as jasper or basalt, that is used to test the quality of gold or silver. A piece of gold or silver is used to mark the touchstone, and the quality of the metal is determined by comparing the streak left on the stone by the metal with a streak made by a standard alloy. If you know how it's supposed to look, you have a shot at knowing whether your gold meets a certain standard.

When we are talking about ideas, the word *touchstone* is used as a basis for comparison, a reference point against which other things can be evaluated. I want you to think of your mission as a touchstone.

For years I didn't really have a touchstone. I just took every day as it came. Sure, I had goals, but goals are temporary, whereas a touchstone is comparative. Think of a touchstone as a standard against which you can judge all of the actions of your life.

So what are the qualities that make you uniquely you? What do you enjoy? What do you want to stand for?

My friend Blake has been to a lot of deathbeds and a lot of funerals. As a pastor, he's often there when it happens. It's that last second, when you look back and ask the question, "Did my life make a difference?" So I asked him, "What's the difference between the people who really made a difference and the people who didn't?" I asked the question because I want to make a difference.

It turns out that it's the little things that count. It's not the big events that people remember at the end; it's the small kindnesses. I know. You aren't shocked. I say it and you know it is true, but do you live that way? Do you take the time to compare what you are doing to the standard you know is true? I didn't. Life is busy. We have things to do, so it's not easy to compare what we do everyday to a standard—or is it?

Earlier I mentioned Jack Canfield's "Life Purpose Exercise," which made it work for me and made all of the difference. The exercise is just four simple questions found in his book *The Success Principles.*

What I got from that process is a touchstone. Each time that I think about taking on a new project, I can compare the project to my touchstone. If I have an opportunity to make a million dollars in poodle beds, does that move me closer to my mission or system objectives? Maybe, but it's not likely. With a clear touchstone, you can evaluate your missions and see if they make sense in the big picture.

After you've clearly identified your mission or the objective(s) of your system, you've essentially made clear which way you'd like to create maximum impact in your life. After that point, you are now ready to dive further into the system creation process and actually start to design your system. Now it's time for the big question:

Do You Want to Build Your Systems Yourself?

You certainly don't have to! As with everything else in your life, you get to choose. Once you are actively thinking about systems you will be able to find them everywhere, and there are lots of ways to put systems together, so that you have your own personal impact system. Here are four techniques you can use:

- Create.
- Purchase.
- Model.
- Hire an expert.

Create.

The first option is just to create systems out of thin air. Look at what you have right now, define your goals, decide what you need, and write down the steps you need to take to make it happen. Note: I don't recommend this option. It can certainly work, but if you aren't following a proven model then you are wasting time. Your personal time can't be replaced.

Purchase.

Here are existing systems that may plug directly into your personal impact system. The key is to make sure that any systems you purchase match your needs. If someone has taken the time to spend hundreds of thousands of dollars developing a shopping cart, it *might* save you time and expense if you can purchase that system for a hundred dollars. Here are some of the trade-offs between building custom system components and purchasing key modules in general:

Custom

- ☐ Usually meet your needs more precisely.
- ☐ Higher initial costs.
- ☐ Easier to learn and use.
- ☐ Simpler.
- ☐ Harder to maintain.
- ☐ Costs to update.

Purchased

- ☐ Less likely to meet your needs precisely.
- ☐ Lower initial costs.
- ☐ May include features that you don't want that require additional time and resources.
- ☐ May have documentation included.
- ☐ More complex.
- ☐ Easier to maintain.
- ☐ May include updates.

Model.

Remember the MTA Action System? One of the most effective ways to build systems is to find existing systems that you see working very well in the marketplace. Then replicate those systems into your system. How are the top 3 percent reaching your audience? Actively look for leaders who have built systems and see how they are creating their own mix of custom and purchased systems. Don't forget, you always have the option to...

Hire an Expert.

At some point, you may want to bring in a real systems expert to help you fine-tune your operation. Seasoned professionals can help you to find the advantages and/or problems that you may have missed.

☐ ☐ ☐

Whether you create from scratch, purchase, model, or hire an expert, you need to know a little about the basics of building your system. It all starts with objects and processes.

Objects

Let's start first with the objects. So your task is to identify all of the objects that are part of or come into contact with your system. As an example, let's say you want to build a Website. You have a goal, so now you sit down to brainstorm all of the objects that may be part of your Website-building system:

- Computer
- Internet
- Keyboard
- Me
- Graphics designer
- Web host server
- Visitors to my Website
- Graphics for my Website
- Autoresponder
- Graphics software
- HTML editing software
- FTP software
- Programmer

Once you have the list, you can determine whether a particular object is integral to your system. What you are doing is defining the boundary of your system. Your system boundary is simply a "fence" that separates those objects inside of your system from those that are outside of your system.

For instance, you might break an autoresponder into two separate objects: autoresponder sign-up form and autoresponder service. The autoresponder form is part of your Website, but the autoresponder service itself is completely separate from your Website and managed by a third party.

Here is one way you might organize your system:

Website-Building System

- ☐ Computer (including computer, monitor, keyboard, mouse)
- ☐ Yourself
- ☐ Graphics for your Website
- ☐ Autoresponder sign-up form
- ☐ Graphics software
- ☐ HTML editing software
- ☐ FTP software

Environment

- ☐ Internet (because it is an external tool that you use)
- ☐ Graphics designer (if you are going to outsource)
- ☐ Web host server
- ☐ Autoresponder service
- ☐ Programmer
- ☐ Visitors to your Website

Processes

After you've identified the objects, the next step is to identify the processes that you need to reach your goal. A process is a series of actions. As you define your system, think of objects as nouns and processes as verbs.

Make another list of all of the things that have to happen in order to reach your goal:

- Graphics designer must design a logo.
- You need to upload a series of messages to your autoresponder.
- The programmer needs to integrate the autoresponder system into your Website by placing an autoresponder form on the sign-up page.

I know that the list seems endless at first, but in order to reach your maximum impact, you need to know all of the objects and processes that will play a part in your success. Because there are so many, you want to make sure that you have a clear system so that you don't miss anything.

The next step is to clearly and systematically document your business processes. If you don't write them down then you forget them. Have you ever experienced a situation where you have a crucial idea in your mind, only to get sidetracked by a phone call, an e-mail, or other distraction? If you don't document your system, you will find yourself racking your brain trying to remember something that was clear to you only moments before.

You may want to carry a journal or a notebook everywhere you go. Any time that we write our thoughts on paper, it helps to solidify our ideas. It's a proven fact that writing something burns it into our mind. When you write your systems down with a focus on the system boundary, subsystems, components, and the processes that act on those objects, you will engrain that system into your mind.

One of the best methods for documenting your system concepts is through the use of process mapping. Process mapping is a technique that enables you to document on paper the objects and processes of your system. The technique forces you to focus on the interrelationships of your objects and processes as well as between the support and core processes that you have identified. Process maps provide you with a method for describing and analyzing the three core components of any system:

- Physical pieces (called objects, components, or subsystems)
- Functions (called processes or activities)
- Interfaces (often referred to as inputs or outputs)

☐ ☐ ☐

Let's do a brief recap!

The functions of a system are the actions or processes that a system performs. A physical component such as a headlamp performs the function: provide light. Similarly, the steering wheel as a component plays a role in the function: steer vehicle.

The third important part of a system involves interfaces. We haven't covered interfaces, but an interface plays an important role in the definition and documenting of your system. Interfaces specify connections between physical pieces, between physical objects and their functions, and between functions. The interfaces specify important information regarding the state of the system such as inputs and outputs between each step of the process.

For process mapping resources and more information on building systems, go to *TheImpactFactor.com/resources/*.

Here are three essential ways in which you'll benefit by employing a systems approach to your business or other life mission:

1. Optimize your own processes.
2. Differentiate your message.
3. Remove yourself.

Optimize Your Own Processes.

Identifying your processes will help you understand the bottlenecks within your personal impact system and enable you to streamline your operations. That means improved throughput, a reduction in waste, and an overall increase in revenue and profitability.

Differentiate Your Message.

Many people focus on providing information. Today, this is not enough. Your audience has access to unlimited information 24 hours per day through the Internet. They don't need more information; what they need is systems that solve their problems. Provide your audience with information, and you may get a sale. Provide them with a system they can replicate on their own, and you'll generate an audience for a lifetime.

Remove Yourself.

It's much easier to replace a team member when you know exactly what he or she is doing, and the documentation makes it much easier to train the new team member. Once you know exactly what it takes to achieve your goals, you can find ways to remove yourself from the system. Start with the elements that required large amounts of your time and move through every process that has the object "You" attached to it. Soon you will find that your entire operation can function and grow without your active participation, but first I want to make sure that you can pay some important bills.

You Can't Make a Difference if You Can't Pay the Bills

Literally every day I receive e-mails from people who sincerely want to make a difference in this world, but are struggling to make it financially. Having great ideas won't save the world if you can't keep the doors open and food on the table. Let's face it: Life just isn't easy, and the amount of money that you have to work with makes a difference in the quality of your life and the quality of the lives that you impact if you use it wisely.

My goal was never to be rich. I've met a lot of unhappy rich people, so I know that wealth alone is not going to make you happy. That said, we all operate better with a little bit of security. I know there are exceptions you can think of right now when you did something amazing because of the fact that you weren't secure, but think for a minute of the countless hours that you have wasted in your life because something broke and you didn't have the money to fix it.

I know that my wife and kids appreciate a little bit of security, and I'm sure that your family won't mind having some either. After all, if you find yourself with too much money, there is always someone to give it to. I'm encouraging you to make sure that you have your finances secure because that is one of the key factors in achieving your maximum impact.

I've tried quite a few ways to make money over the years. I've been an employee, I've owned a business, I've owned real estate, and I've invested in the stock market, and they all have advantages and disadvantages. For this chapter I'm going to make a couple of assumptions, and, if my assumptions don't fit you, feel free to disregard the chapter or take what ideas you can.

First, I'm going to assume that you have an entrepreneurial spirit. Even if you don't necessarily want to own a business of your own, I can tell by the fact that you are reading this book that you are thinking creatively towards building your own ideas and moving them through the world. That requires that you think as an entrepreneur, even if you are working within a corporate structure.

Second, I'm going to assume that we are going to work together to build your personal impact and that you will want to build revenue streams in order to expand your impact.

One of the joys of hosting the jvAlert Live events is that I get to watch lots of new people launching new products and becoming positioned as experts in their fields. It's pretty amazing how quickly you can become a "household name" in the Internet Age.

But, some of these people are still struggling. They have their five-figure launches and get a little famous, and their fans think that everything must be perfect for them. In reality, they finish their big launch, and then the headaches start. Huge percentages go to affiliates and partners, expenses, and support. Returns start coming in and suddenly you are wondering why you did this at all. What's worse, you have to get up the next day and do it all again, because the bills didn't stop and you can't either, and so it goes, product launch after product launch.

I was luckier than most and fell into an amazing secret from the time of my first big success. This single secret saved my business for sure and probably my marriage, because, without some security, family life can get really tense. The simple secret? Recurring revenue. Recurring revenue is income that keeps coming to you every month. The magic bullet of recurring revenue is the fact that you make the sale once, but you continue to get paid. There are countless examples of recurring income models.

Have You Ever Had a Gym Membership?

At every gym, there is a core group of dedicated people who religiously go to the gym every week, but they are in the minority. Most people who sign up for a gym membership have great intentions of going on a regular basis—and most of them don't. In fact, if they did go on a regular basis it would probably be a very crowded gym. Hard to believe, but some of the people who have gym memberships never go at all. So why don't they cancel their memberships? Eventually some of them do, but a significant percentage of them don't cancel their memberships because they think they might go again soon.

Gyms are expensive to build and maintain, and if the gym charged by the hour for each visit it would be very expensive. The regulars would have a tough time paying for it. The people who don't work out regularly would never pay it, and the gym would go out of business. As it is, the people who own the gym and the people who do work out on a regular basis are subsidized by the people who only come in infrequently.

From the gym's standpoint, the cash flow is much more consistent too, which is another reason that you want to build recurring revenue streams into your personal impact system.

An Author's Recurring Income System

Here's an example of a great recurring income system for an author who has a message to share with the world:

- Articles
- Blog
- E-mail list
- E-book
- Podcast
- Interviews
- Viral videos
- Member community
- Book
- Print newsletter
- Licensing of materials
- CD/DVD
- Monthly Webcast
- LockIn software
- Speaking engagements
- Mastermind groups

- High-end coaching
- Outbound call center
- Live events and workshops

Getting Started

Let's say that Sally has been writing articles about her passion for ages and finally put up her own blog. As a first step, Sally starts repurposing those old articles, adding her credentials and a link to her blog at the bottom of each article. Then she starts submitting the articles to article directories online and print magazines. That's a start at least.

Over time, people see Sally's articles and she starts getting a little traffic to her blog. She captures names and e-mail addresses on her blog and puts them into an autoresponder system so that she can automatically send them a series of messages about what she is doing.

Sally decides to compile some of the information from her articles and blog postings into an e-book, which she sells on the Internet for $39. She adds the sales page to her autoresponder series, posts on the blog and talks about it in the podcast. She gets a few sales, but certainly not enough to make a living off of. Meanwhile, she decides to do some short audio recordings of key points from her articles and post them on a podcast.

Another expert in her field noticed her blog and signed up to her e-mail list. When Sally started doing her podcast, the expert asked if she could interview Sally for her own list. Sally did the interview and mentioned her blog and podcast on the interview.

Adding Value

Sally realizes that she can add some extra value and generate some interest to her blog by creating a funny video that highlights some of the disasters that can occur if you don't think about her subject. Throughout the video, viewers are shown the link to the blog and promised a preview version of Sally's e-book. Sally uses a simple software program to automate the process of submitting her video to dozens of sites and podcast directories. Because Sally's videos are hilarious, people start sending them to friends.

Sally invests some more time to create additional videos, and the traffic starts pouring in. Sally decides that it's time to get some real credentials and authority by using her existing materials to write a solid book.

Using Leverage

As she writes the book, she leverages everything that she has learned about public relations, networks, and key influencers to build important relationships. She also creates a membership site for prospects interested in the book and develops content for members only, with two membership levels available. There is a free-level membership and a gold-level membership that costs $39 per month and includes additional videos and downloadable materials.

Sally knows that her book is really a business card for driving people to her products, so she takes the time to do a full publicity build-up for the book launch.

Modeling the Best

Sally manages to model successful authors and, by leveraging her impact skills, she makes her book a modest best-seller. In the process, she generates more than 5,000 free members and 200 paid members to her membership site. The recurring membership alone gives her a monthly income of $7,800 each month. Each month some members quit and others are added, but the average member stays for at least four months.

During the four months, Sally works hard at providing value and adds a platinum-level membership with all of the benefits of the gold-level membership, plus a monthly printed newsletter, a CD of one of her podcasts and a monthly teleconference mastermind session with only "platinum" members invited, for $75 per month; 25 of her "gold" members upgrade immediately.

Adding Staff

At this point, Sally needs a virtual assistant to help with customer questions and other tasks, so she hires an assistant to work 10 hours per week. The assistant also helps to line up joint venture partners, and, working with key partners, Sally decides to create a home study course from her materials and augment it with materials from her partners.

Because of the quality of her materials, Sally is able to convince several partners to integrate her materials into their existing products and pay her a percentage of sales. Her partners are also raising her visibility through regular promotions and the fact that she is featured in their own materials.

Building Reputation

With her growing credentials as a published author and the social proof created by constant endorsement by respected professionals, Sally is regularly asked to speak at industry events. With the successful creation of her home-study course, Sally has product available to sell at events, so she starts by speaking at a few events and offering a pre-release version of her home-study course to attendees only. Sally systematically collects testimonials from all of the purchasers of her course and assembles case studies as proof that her system works.

With the help of her growing team and helpful partners who she has cultivated at live events, Sally launches her home-study course and generates hundreds of thousands of dollars in the period of a single week. Now everyone knows who Sally is, because her name has been everywhere.

High-End Offerings

Sally is perfectly positioned to begin offering a high-end coaching program, workshops, and other live events.

Notice that Sally didn't do everything that she could have done. No one can do everything. But look at the massive impact that she has already had, and it is just beginning. Even more importantly, Sally has the recurring financial base to allow her to continue to grow her impact.

Living Without You

To create impact bigger than yourself, you must make sure your impact can grow without you. The more you see yourself in your plan, the smaller the impact. If you can get out of the way, your impact will move beyond your dreams.

You are already well on your way to creating your own system for creating massive impact and the possibilities are endless. Here are just a few of the things that you can do to increase your impact:

- Write a book.
- Speak.
- Coach.
- Mentor.
- Public relations.
- Copywriting.
- Partner recruitment.
- Advertising.
- Interviews.
- Work with non-profit organizations.
- Belong to associations.
- Become an expert.
- Search engine optimization.
- Magazine articles.
- Host live events.

- Host a radio show.
- Produce a television show.
- Create information products.
- Manage affiliates.
- Create viral software.
- Create a Website.
- Maintain a blog.
- Direct mail.
- Postcards.
- Teleconferences.
- Webcasts.
- Sponsorships.
- Grants.
- Certification programs.
- And much, much more.

So for just a moment imagine that you have built your system, and you have all of the key elements in it. You've really busted your chops and done it all. You've worked nights, weekends, and early mornings, and stolen precious moments from your family and friends for months, but it's finally all put together.

You have a Website, a publisher for your new book, and a coaching system that you've spent months developing. You've created a home-study course for your back-end product and a recurring income continuity program that helps you get your message out. Your publicity is ready for the huge launch that you are planning. You have radio and TV interviews set, not to mention a book tour, Webcasts, and a possible television show of your own. It's time to sit back and enjoy your success, right?

Famous Last Words

"Plenty of time to sleep on day 91."

—Sterling Valentine

When Sterling Valentine was eating ramen noodles and existing on three to four hours of sleep a night as he struggled to pull everything together for his massive *Joint Venture Formula* launch on day 90 during his 90-day challenge, he kept telling me that he could sleep on day 91. I kept telling Sterling that all hell breaks loose on day 91.

Planning for Success

> "If you think you are busy now, just wait until massive success starts rolling in."
>
> —Ken McArthur

The natural instinct is to try to do everything yourself. As you become more and more successful, you realize that you've put tremendous amounts of time and energy into creating your impact. If you look at the organizational chart for your impact system, you probably see you, you, you, you, you, and you.

Most people who set out to make a difference in the world make the mistake of thinking that they are the sole person responsible for making it happen. Luckily, there are people to help, and that prospect list you've been building is a good place to start looking for them.

Building Your Team

Maximum impact doesn't happen on your own. One of the most crucial factors in getting high levels of impact is recruiting the very best possible team to work with. Team members can be employees, partners, apprentices, or even your customers. Bottom line: You need these people.

Personally, I want a lifestyle that allows me to choose when and where I work. When I started to get serious about building my own team, I decided to work only with the very best. That was a problem because, when I was starting out, I didn't have a lot of cash flow to pay the very best. Besides, it's not easy to know who the very best people are.

Have you ever hired an employee with great expectations for success and then found out within the first month that he or she just wasn't going to work out? I certainly have, and it's not a pretty picture. By the time that I'd decided to actively build a team, I already knew that employees weren't my best option. There were several reasons in addition to the cash flow issue.

For one thing, my office was in my basement, and my wife wasn't too thrilled about having employees coming to the house every day. I tend to think that Internet-marketing–savvy people are all over the place, but that's because I live in an online community of people who are working on the Internet. Most people aren't Internet-savvy. If you are an Internet marketer, try telling your neighbor what you do for a living. Most people just think scammer and spammer when they think of Internet marketing.

I decided that my team needed to be a virtual team. Working with a virtual team allows team members to come from anywhere in the world, and that broadens the base of people who are available. Virtual team members also have the advantage of having their own freedom and flexibility as long as they can get the job done. After all, getting the job done is what it's all about. I want to reward the team based on results.

A Real Apprentice Program

I'd seen other marketers offer paid apprentice programs—people often pay an expert to help them learn the business—so I decided to offer my own mentoring program. I looked at other mentoring programs, did my homework, and put my ideas together. I worked hard on a dynamic sales letter that I thought nailed the benefits and sent it to thousands of prospects. What were my results? Not a single person responded to my offer.

I felt bad. Here I had all of this knowledge and success. I knew that I could help people, and no one wanted what I was offering. It was time to eat humble pie, so I gave up on charging people for the moment, and I sent out this simple e-mail to my prospects:

> Dear (Prospect First Name),
>
> I need some help in my business because I just don't have time in the day to do it all and I really don't want to hire an "employee."
>
> What if I teach you one of my businesses from the ground up in return for you doing the day-to-day work?
>
> The worse case is that you get to see how everything works in the "real world" and the best case is that I see what a great job you can do.

At that point, maybe we can work out some kind of deal
where you can run that business and take home a share
of the profits from a business that's been around for
years and has sold millions of dollars in sales.

If you want to give it a try, e-mail me at *ken@jvAlert.com.*

There's nothing to lose, but your time.

Let me know what you think.

All the best,
Ken

Immediately, I had dozens of responses. Jason Mangrum, a friend and
Internet marketer, got my e-mail and offered to send my e-mail out to his
list, too, and soon there were more than 100 people interested in working
with me. What was I going to do with 100 people?

No Time to Train

I was already completely overworked, trying to do it all on my own,
and, to tell you the truth, I really didn't have time to train and manage a
100-person team. That much was obvious, but what wasn't obvious was
what to do.

Now I had 100 people who were waiting, so I decided to hold a teleconference. I planned to talk to the people who responded, explain the
situation that I had, and see what happened.

I know, it's hard to believe, but 100 people didn't come to the teleconference. No matter what the response is for any offer, you can count on
some people just going away. For some of them it was a bad time, so I
posted a recording. Others just didn't show up. That was a good thing.
About 34 people total actually signed up for the program and decided that
they wanted to participate in the program.

At the time, one of my biggest time-eaters was Affiliate Showcase customer support. You can imagine that, with 40,000 plus customers, there
was plenty of support to handle, so the first thing that I told my new apprentices was that I wanted them to start learning about the Affiliate Showcase part of my business.

Sid Hale wrote an amazing book called the *Insider's Guide to Affiliate
Showcase,* a massive document that explained everything that you ever

wanted to know about Affiliate Showcase and how to use it to generate profits. Sid was kind enough to donate a copy of the book to every one of my new apprentices.

At the time, one of the front-line support vehicles for Affiliate Showcase was the member forums. My support plan at the time was first to encourage all of my members to use those forums 24 hours a day to help each other with questions that they might have. That allowed me to outsource some of my customer support directly to the members and give them faster responses at the same time. If they couldn't get questions answered there, then they could contact our customer support department. (At the time the customer support department was...me.)

My apprentices' first task was to join the Affiliate Showcase forums and to read Sid Hale's *Insider's Guide to Affiliate Showcase*. I also gave them a free copy of the site to play with and use on their own, and I told them to start answering questions about Affiliate Showcase in the forums. Then I told them that I was going to watch them. What I was looking for was a "superstar," and I wanted them to know that I was looking.

By the second week, the participants were starting to settle into clear layers. At the bottom layer were the people who hadn't done a thing. That was a healthy number of people. Taking action is the most difficult—and most crucial—thing people ever have to do.

The next layer was people who started reading and thinking and thinking and thinking. I see this all the time. We love to study and learn and think. Sometimes we spend all of our time taking actions and still get nowhere. We start thinking, and that just confuses us more and more. We learn and explore, and then we take more action to learn and think, but in the end we accomplish nothing.

The next layer was people who read the book, made a few posts in response to questions in the forums, and were ready for the next step. How often have you waited to find out what the next step is? We do it all the time! I see this behavior most often in a special group of people. What makes these people unique is that way that they approach a task.

How Do You Approach a Task?

Some people go step-by-step. If you give them instructions to build a bookcase, they will be fine as long as nothing goes wrong. So, if you want to build a box...

Step 1:　Remove pieces from the box.

Step 2:　Place Section A at a 45-degree angle to Section B.

Step 3:　Screw Section A to Section B.

Oops, there is a screw missing! Now what do I do?

Other people see the parts and just start putting them together. If you don't have a screw, you think of 20 other ways to put two boards together and make them stick. Maybe you use glue, maybe you nail it, and maybe it isn't pretty, but when you are done you definitely have a bookcase. Stepwise people find it more difficult to adjust to unknown situations, and when you are building impact, almost everything is unknown.

Don't get me wrong. Stepwise people are wonderful, and the best way to create a team is to make sure that you have both stepwise and creative thinkers on your team. If you put together a team of people that only think creatively, they will come up with thousands of original ideas—and implement none of them. If you put two stepwise people together they will be hopelessly blocked at the first problem.

Of course, this is an exaggeration. All of us are creative and organized. We have to be. But, everyone has a preference, and if you match complimentary modes you can have some amazing results. I would be totally lost without someone to keep me on track and moving to the next step.

Superstars

The top layer is the "superstar" layer that I told my apprentices I would be looking for. Alysan Delaney-Childs was a superstar from the day she responded to my offer. Within days, Alysan knew Affiliate Showcase inside and out. She responded to customers with clearly thought-out answers, and she was helping other apprentices to get started. Initiative is a wonderful thing.

Don't think that Alysan was a beginner. Alysan already had a formal business education, a ton of experience, and great contacts within the industry, and she could have been spending time building her own business. So why was she volunteering as an unpaid apprentice? Clearly, Alysan saw the value in learning the systems that make a successful business operate. If you ask her now, I'm sure that she will tell you that it was well worth her investment. By the way, if you want to learn a business, a true apprentice position allows you to model success, and that's a value that's priceless.

I wanted to see just far how Alysan could go, so I decided to give her more responsibilities. Alysan was already helping the rest of the apprentices, so I put her in charge of the entire customer support team for Affiliate Showcase. Now she was off to the races.

Beyond the Basics

Sterling Valentine's project started to require large amounts of my time and I was developing *Info Product Blueprint* and planning for the next jvAlert Live event. These twin activities were barely leaving me time to breath. I clearly needed tons of help on the jvAlert Live event, so I gathered another group of volunteers to help with that project and put Alysan in charge as the team leader.

One of the key parts of the *Info Product Blueprint* project was a massive workbook in which I planned to cover every aspect of creating, promoting, and profiting from info products. The problem was that life was getting a little crazy, and there was just no more of me.

As we'd hoped, jvAlert Live was a roaring success, Sterling Valentine shared his triumph with a crowd of admiring fans, and Alysan ran a tight ship as she led her team and all of the attendees though an amazing event. Fresh off her success with managing the jvAlert Live event, I put Alysan in charge of managing the entire *Info Product Blueprint* project. Together we enlisted the help of Dan Giordano, one of the attendees at jvAlert Live and an experienced marketing professional, who we put in charge of editing the workbook.

All together, the team leaders compiled a list of more than 50 contributors, and convinced them to join the project team and contribute materials to our project. All of the contributors were seasoned experts who lived, ate, and breathed their subjects. We knew that we were getting the best of the best, and the resulting workbook alone was more than 650 pages.

To support the apprentices, volunteers, and contributors, we put together a team of professionals to help with the *Info Product Blueprint Launch* product creation and launch logistics. The team included Michelle Alvarez, who was in charge of all of our workbook production, editing, and transcripts, and Becky Dielman, who helped to pull together the Website. Karl Barndt and Ray Edwards were instrumental in the copywriting department, and Ben Blakesley was our amazing sound engineer. In fact, every person on the team was amazing.

Here's what the finished package included:

Section One: **The Making of Joint Venture Formula (complete 6 DVD set)**

This DVD set documents how I helped Sterling Valentine go from an Internet marketing rookie with no product, no partners, and no large mailing list to an " instant" Internet marketing celebrity. Now you can see the entire process, behind the scenes, documented "as it happened."

Section Two: **Skill Set DVDs (complete 8 DVD set)**

- Launching With Style—Mike Filsaime
- Copywriting Basics—Carl Galletti
- Internet Infomercials 101—Mike Koenigs
- Selling Your Products—John Di Lemme
- Photography for Info Products—Mary Mazullo
- The 7 Steps for Creating Remarkable Projects—Michael Port
- Two Complete DVDs on Outsourcing Info Product Creation—Frank Sousa

Section Three: **Skill Set Audio CDs (complete 6 CD set, with full printed transcripts)**

- Using Audio and Video to Sell Info Products—Rick Raddatz
- Selling Info Products on eBay—Mike Enos
- Building Content for Info Products—Lori Steffen & Jeff Wark
- Customer Service for Info Products—JoAnna Brandi
- How Live Seminars and Events Help You Create and Sell Info Products—Mike Ambrosio
- Legal Issues to Consider When Creating and Selling Info Products—Bob Silber

Section Four:　　**Case Study Audio CDs (complete 5 CD set, with full printed transcripts)**

- Surefire Marketing Launches—Yanik Silver
- The Affiliate Manager Launch—Anik Singal
- Super Affiliate Handbook Launch—Rosalyn Gardner
- Wedding Firesale Launch—Willie Crawford
- E-book Launch—Frank Sousa

Section Five:　　**Massive 673-page, Comprehensive Info Product Blueprint Workbook and Action Plan**

☐ ☐ ☐

Now stop for a minute and count up the number of people that it took to create *Info Product Blueprint.* Notice that I didn't even mention the people who helped with photography, graphics, fulfillment, or our complete marketing team.

Nevertheless, you get the idea. This wasn't a one-person project. I didn't have a spare second, much less the countless hours that it took to produce this amazing product myself.

To start building my team and create my product, I sent out a single very simple e-mail.

You Can't Do Everything.

Here are some things I didn't do:

- Organize it.
- Recruit the experts.
- Write the workbook.
- Edit the materials.
- Edit the sound.
- Create the graphics.
- Format materials.
- Put up the Website.
- Integrate the shopping cart.

- Manufacture the product.
- Take the orders.
- Track the shipments.

You Don't Need to Know Everything.

I didn't even have to know everything there was to know about creating and marketing information products, because I had more than 50 top-level experts that gave me their best materials.

Now I can hear you saying, "But Ken, I'm not a high-powered industry leader. I'm just starting out, and there is no way that 50 people are going to help me out." Well, you are wrong about that. I've seen it happen countless times with people who come to our "Get Your Product Done" workshop and to jvAlert Live events.

Here's one final thought that I'll share with you. I don't mention it a lot, but it's important that you know, because I want you to realize that you can build an amazing team of dedicated people who will stand by you, and even lead your movement to create massive impact.

Info Product Blueprint was the first very first info product that I ever produced. That should let you know that you don't have to think small when you start creating your own impact. If you think big enough, you can make your own launches much bigger than mine ever were. After all, I was stumbling around trying to make a difference. At the time, I had no system at all. But you are a long way ahead of that. I just gave you a great system for building a team. All you need to do is give yourself permission to fly.

If you want help forming your own team, visit our resource center at *TheImpactFactor.com/resources/*.

Beyond One Life

I n the first chapter, I told you how a series of choices made by a single spider led to the shattering of A.J. Velichko's fragile neck. I also promised to tell you the rest of the story. Fortunately, the story is not over. It is just beginning. A.J. has touched the lives of countless people and will continue to touch even more every day of his life. Even today, A.J.'s story is reaching out to you and touching your life, and it never would have happened if it weren't for a series of little choices.

Little Things Make a Difference.

The simple choices that spider made changed A.J.'s life and the lives of everyone who knows him. The spider didn't get up one day and think, "I'm going to go out and change hundreds of lives." It was just a series of simple questions. Do I go right or left? Do I go up or down? It was a tiny decision in a busy life, made by a small spider.

You have so much more say in the world than that simple spider has. Today you get to make the choice to change the world, and, unlike the spider, you get to make your impact grow. You see, the spider made its decision and the world went on. There were no follow-up actions. It didn't focus in on creating ways that its message was clear or repeatable. It didn't even have a message to spread.

But you are different. You can solve real problems in this world. You can fine-tune your message. You can get your ideas, products,

231

and services noticed. You can motivate millions of people to spread the word about what you are doing. You can identify the networks that your audience exists in right now and the key influencers within those networks. You can build systems to spread the word automatically that efficiently keep supporting the people you want to help. You can launch your ideas with intensity, focus, and social proof, and you can build a platform of recurring income that can sustain your impact beyond one life.

Right now you may be feeling small, but imagine the impact that one small spider had and tell me that you haven't gained the tools that take you beyond your dreams. As Anita Roddick, author of *Business as Unusual: My Entrepreneurial Journey,* says, "If you think you're too small to have an impact, try going to bed with a mosquito in the room."

The days, weeks, and months that A.J. spent in hospital rooms were hard, to say the least. Of course he wondered why—who wouldn't? Sometimes he was feeling beyond down, but each day he lived he affected more and more people.

It was tough. His mother was a single mom, working hard to make ends meet. A.J. suddenly could do nothing for himself, and she had to be there for him constantly. The medical bills were piling up. If you've ever looked at a hospital bill for a single day, you have an idea of what it was like. Except it wasn't a one-day stay. It went on month after month.

The people in his church thought that they were helping to give A.J. courage as they rallied to try to help with the unbelievable medical expenses. They created a series of fundraisers that barely put a dent in the bills, but it wasn't so much that they were helping A.J. The truth was that A.J. was inspiring them.

As the people in the community tried so hard to help, he taught them that life was hard, but that amazing things can happen. We can do so little alone and so much together. Life is more than we ever imagined. Courage, faith, and hope can see us through so much more than we believe.

At first, it was impossible to know if there was any chance at all. Paralyzed from the neck down, he was trapped in a "halo" neckpiece and unable to move. Nevertheless, each day A.J. took small simple actions and very slowly reclaimed his body one small movement at a time.

I remember the days his mother stood up in church to tell us about his progress: the day he first sat upright in the bed, the day he stood, the day he walked, and finally the day that he danced. All that time, A.J. didn't know what the future held for him. He didn't know when the progress might end. All he had were possibilities for an amazing future.

I hope that this book has given you a small hint of what is possible for you. You have an unlimited ability to make a difference. But, it is just a hint. What will actually happen is so amazing it is completely incomprehensible. Each life you touch touches another, and so it grows. Every kindness you give or hateful action that you take, spreads throughout our world.

Let Me Prove It to You.

It is undeniable. We are interconnected. Our words move at light speed and what you choose to do affects thousands, even if you don't want it to.

When I was growing up, my father was what they called a mobile minister. In my elementary and junior high days, he served the small communities in southwestern Colorado, traveling as much as 200 miles on a Sunday and preaching to bean farmers, oil field workers, fire spotters, and the few people left in the high mining towns. I don't know if he knew the difference that he was making, but I did. His heart was golden, and I could tell even at that young age that he was changing people's lives, one life at a time. Each life that he touched affected other lives.

My mother was a rock. She convinced me that I could do anything and she fiercely defended all her children from anyone who even hinted that their possibilities were not endless. I was fortunate. Every day the people in my life did little things that showed me that I had real value and that what we do makes a difference.

For many people, it's not that way. Your parents may have been cold and uncaring. They may have cut you down at every opportunity. They may have wished that you didn't exist and abused you physically or emotionally. But, if there is any speck of human kindness, love, or caring within your body and mind, someone did something to put it there.

Think about who those people are for a moment. Remember someone who was kind to you and changed your life. How different would your life be if he or she hadn't made the effort?

Parents often find themselves listening to their kids as they act out and rebel. They wonder, "Where did they get that idea? Where did that come from?" The truth is that it came from another person. The simple actions that another person took affected what your children think, say, and do.

Every day the actions that you take affect the people around you. That includes every kind word and every sarcastic comment. It is scary to think about, because at some point you can't take it back anymore. How many marriages have ended because at some point one little thing was said that broke the camel's back?

You may not see the people you change, so I'd like to encourage you to take a second to measure your impact on the world. If you measure how your life touches others, you will see that you have the ability, skills and resources to affect millions of people.

Metrics are the ways that we measure results into quantitative numbers over time. As people, we need the numbers—real numbers. Metrics are important because we "think" that we know many things but, when we start measuring the actual results, we find out that we are often wrong.

Today, it is crucial that you start measuring your impact, so that you see yourself moving toward your clearly defined goals. That's why I created the "Beyond One Life" research project, because it is important that you see and measure the impact that you have on countless people around you.

Try to imagine a football game where no one keeps score. It wouldn't be much fun, would it? In a football game, you want to cheer for someone, and you need the score to let you know how your team is doing. I am cheering for you—not from the sidelines, but from the middle of the huddle. I want to call out the yard markers as I see you moving toward the goal posts, and I want the people in the stands to rise to their feet as they see the scoreboard blazing out the numbers in bright lights that prove decisively that you have won this difficult but thrilling challenge.

Here's the way we tend to think life works:

You go to work and you do your job. You aren't outstanding, but you aren't awful either. You come home to your spouse and you are tired. Sometimes you're cranky, but most times you work things out. It's frustrating. You are surviving financially, but can't ever seem to get ahead. Whatever you make is what it takes, and you feel yourself slowly going deeper into debt. You feel that you aren't making any difference at all, and sometimes you wonder if it's worth it. You hope for the future but try not to get your hopes up too high, because you know that it never works out the way that you plan. Opportunities are fewer and fewer, and problems seem to rise by the hour. Each little thing that goes wrong seems as if it's the last straw. You just can't seem to get a break. Things are slowly falling apart.

Here's how life can work:

Each day you wake up and take small actions that move you closer to your goals. Each day you experience small but steady progress. At the end of the day, you ask yourself, "Did I live my life? Did I take a chance? Did I make a difference? Did I love? Did I give?" Some days you aren't so perfect, but each day you measure. At the end of a week, you can see your progress and you can say, without reservation, "YES!"

Measuring your impact can change your life. Countable results keep you going when you think that the world's problems are so big that you can never make a difference. People change the world every day, but someone needs to remind them constantly. Sure, some problems are difficult, but there are real solutions to problems out there. People solve problems every day, and most of the time we don't notice at all.

Today I want to challenge you to do three things:

1. Make a difference you can measure.

2. Share your experience with others.

3. Help me start something big.

People can feel your impact in every school, university, business, and non-profit organization in the world. Can you teach others? Can you spread the word? You know that together we can change millions of lives.

Imagine a world where we can all inspire each other to create a positive and measurable impact. Envision a world where people can no longer deny the responsibility that we all hold as we influence each other in amazing, positive, and giving ways, because undeniable proof is sitting in front of our very eyes. You have the power to create powerful proof that your life matters and you can make a difference.

You Can Help Positively Affect the Lives of 1 Billion People.

Think about that number for a minute. If you can impact one person's life every second of every day, it will only take 31 years to impact a billion people. But, remember the many ways that we can generate exponential results. You will see exactly how long it takes, and you will be amazed.

BeyondOneLife.com is a bold new experiment to measure the ways that we make a difference and to show that impact in a powerful way that will encourage you to grow your impact beyond one life.

Imagine a graphical search engine for people. As you type your own name, the computer displays a small picture with your name in a circle. Radiating out from your circle are connections with arrows pointing to other circles. If you click on an arrow, a window opens so that you can read the story of how you impacted someone.

It feels good to know that you made a difference, so you click on that person's circle to learn more about him or her. Radiating out from their circle are the connections to people that they have impacted. There are thousands upon thousands of interconnected circles. The circles and connections are almost endless, just as the affect that we have on others is endless.

But *BeyondOneLife.com* is so much more. *BeyondOneLife.com* is an amazing tool and community where you can:

- Discover how everyday people are impacting the world right now.

- Measure your own impact.

- Network with others who share your goals.

- Find partners and key influencers.

- Get your ideas noticed and get your message out.

- Connect with non-profit organizations.

- Get corporate sponsors for your projects.

- Find people who are in the top 3 percent in your own niche.

- Increase your skills.

- Get expert advice.

- Collect testimonials and endorsements.

- Build your own personal impact system.

- And more.

BeyondOneLife.com is a bold new experiment to let people know how one simple action can change the lives of many.

You can inspire others to do the same. Join our community in an exciting, bold, new experiment, and tell the world about the amazing impact that you are having. Your success story can positively affect the lives of one billion people.

To share your own story and be inspired by the countless ways that we impact each other, register right now for your free membership at *BeyondOneLife.com.*

Your life will be amazing.

T his section gives you additional places to find detailed information on subjects covered in this book. New information is available every day, so for the latest comprehensive list of resources, visit the Impact Factor Resource Center at *TheImpactFactor.com/resources/*.

The Resource Center offers more than 100 hours worth of free audio instruction from some of the top marketing experts in the world to teach you—in incredible detail—comprehensive cutting-edge information to increase your personal impact.

All of these audio lessons are from top-level Internet marketing experts including Nathan Anderson, Phil Basten, Kevin Bidwell, Anthony Blake, Mike Chen, Joel R. Christopher, Holly Cotter, Jason Cox, Willie Crawford, Paulette Ensign, Michael T. Glaspie, Carl Galletti, Rosalind Gardner, David Garfinkel, Frank Garon, Randy Gilbert, Darryl Graham, Sid Hale, Doug Hudiburg, Jack Humphrey, Andy Jenkins, Gary Knuckles, Dr. Jeffrey Lant, James Maduk, Jason Mangrum, Jane Mark, Ken McArthur, George McKenzie, Paul Myers, Dr. Neil Shearing, Anik Singal, Jeff Smith, Damon Smith, Kim Thomas, Peter Twist, Bryan Voiles, Ramon Williamson, and Eric Wyson.

Here are some of the topics that are covered:

- How to Get Noticed in a World That Doesn't Want to Listen to You.
- How to Motivate Millions Based on Over 100 Years of Scientific Research.

- How to Change Peoples Lives Using Time-Tested Persuasion Techniques.
- How to Make a Real Difference in the World, One Person at a Time.
- How to Stomp the Search Engines.
- How to Build Search Engine Optimization That Works.
- How to Write Effective Copy That Can Double Your Profits.
- How to Make Amazing Profits From Niche Markets.
- How to Create Products That Sell.
- How to Get Reciprocal Linking.
- How to Make Yourself the Obvious Expert.
- How to Brand Your Brilliance.
- How to Make Money From Blogs.
- How to Get Free Publicity for Your Products and Services.
- How to Build Your List by the Thousands.
- How to Make Money From Affiliate Programs.
- How to Take Joint Ventures Beyond the Basics.
- How to Create Bread and Butter Niche Products.
- How to Use Multi-Media to Increase Your Sales.
- How to Use Booklets For Increased Profits.
- How to Make Your Book a Best-Seller on Amazon.
- And much more.

The Resource Center lists updated links for all of the online resources listed in this book, along with many additional online and offline resources, plus an extensive recommended reading list.

Here are some online resources to get you started right now:

Affiliate Marketing

Affiliate Showcase Affiliate Program Directory and Search Engine

AffiliateShowcase.com

Authoring

Books Mean Credibility

www.booksmeancredibility.com/vip/15

Coaching and Mentoring
Ken McArthur's Coaching and Mentoring Programs
TheImpactFactor.com/coaching

Joint Ventures
jvAlert – Joint Venture Alert System
jvAlert.com/invite.aspx?id=1

Market Research
MBS Internet Research Center
mbsinternet.net

Marketing Forums
Ken McArthur's Impact Marketing Forums
ImpactMarketingForums.com

Marketing Newsletters and Blogs
Ken McArthur's The Impact Factor
TheImpactFactor.com/blog

Ken McArthur's Marketing Thoughts
LearningFolder.net/blog

Outsourcing
The Ultimate Outsource Directory
www.ultimateoutsourcedirectory.com/?rid=34

Product Creation
Info Product Blueprint
InfoProductBlueprint.com

Clear Impact Media
ClearImpactMedia.com

Workshops and Seminars
jvAlert Live – Joint Venture Events
jvAlertLive.com

Get Your Product Done – Product Development Workshops
GetYourProductDone.com

Ken McArthur's Help Desk
McArthur Business Systems, Inc.
MyHelpButton.com/HelpDesk/

Recommended Reading List

Anderson, Chris. *The Long Tail: Why the Future of Business is Selling Less of More.* New York: Hyperion, 2006.

Barron, David R., and Danek S. Kaus. *Power Persuasion: Using Hypnotic Influence to Win In Life, Love And Business.* Bandon, Oreg.: Robert D. Reed Publishers, 2005.

Briggs, Rex, and Greg Stuart. *What Sticks: Why Most Advertising Fails and How to Guarantee Yours Succeeds.* New York: Kaplan Business, 2006.

Burchard, Brendon. *Life's Golden Ticket: An Inspirational Novel.* New York: HarperOne, 2007. .

Canfield, Jack, and Janet Switzer. *The Success Principles* ™: *How to Get from Where You Are to Where You Want to Be.* New York: HarperCollins Publishers, 2007.

Canfield, Jack, Mark Victor Hansen, and Leslie Hewitt. *The Power of Focus.* London: Ebury Press, 2001.

Carnegie, Dale. *How to Win Friends & Influence People.* New York: Pocket Books, 1998.

Chandler, Steve. *100 Ways to Motivate Yourself: Change Your Life Forever.* Franklin Lakes, N.J.: Career Press, 2004.

Chandler, Steve, and Scott Richardson. *100 Ways to Motivate Others: How Great Leaders Can Produce Insane Results Without Driving People Crazy.* Franklin Lakes, N.J.: Career Press, 2004.

Cialdini, Robert B. *Influence: The Psychology of Persuasion.* New York: HarperCollins Publishers, 2007.

Collier, R. *Robert Collier Letter Book.* Old Tappan, N.J.: Prentice Hall Trade (Pearson Education), 2000.

Collins, Jim. *Good to Great: Why Some Companies Make the Leap...and Others Don't.* New York: HarperCollins Publishers, 2001.

Comaford-Lynch, Christine. *Rules for Renegades: How to Make More Money, Rock Your Career, and Revel in Your Individuality.* New York: McGraw-Hill, 2007.

Comm, Joel. *The AdSense Code: What Google Never Told You About Making Money with AdSense.* Garden City, N.Y.: Morgan James Publishing, 2006.

Conger, Jay. *The Necessary Art of Persuasion (HBR OnPoint Enhanced Edition).* Boston: Harvard Business Review (PDF download), 2008.

Dawkins, Richard. *The Selfish Gene.* Oxford: Oxford University Press, 1990.

Dawson, Roger. *Secrets of Power Persuasion for Salespeople.* Franklin Lakes, N.J.: Career Press, 2004.

Dietzel, Glenn. *Author & Grow Rich: How to Author a Book in 12 Hours of Actual Writing Time.* Garden City, N.Y.: Morgan James Publishing, 2007.

Dilenschneider, Robert L. *Power and Influence: Mastering the Art of Persuasion.* Indianapolis: Prentice Hall Professional Technical Reference, 1991.

Dillard, James Price (Editor), and Michael W. Pfau (Editor). *The Persuasion Handbook: Developments in Theory and Practice.* Thousand Oaks, Calif.: SAGE Publications, 2002.

Donovan, Jim. *Handbook to a Happier Life: A Simple Guide to Creating the Life You've Always Wanted.* Novato, Calif.: New World Library, 2003.

——. *This Is Your Life, Not a Dress Rehearsal.* Upper Black Eddy, Pa.: Bovan Publishing Group, 1998.

D'Vari, Marisa. *Building Buzz: How To Reach And Impress Your Target Audience.* Franklin Lakes, N.J.: Career Press, 2004.

Eldridge, Elsom, and Mark Eldridge. *How to Position Yourself as the Obvious Expert: Turbocharge Your Consulting or Coaching Business Now!* Winter Springs, Fla.: MasterMind Publishing, LLC, 2004.

Ferriss, Timothy. *The 4-Hour Workweek: Escape 9-5, Live Anywhere, and Join the New Rich.* New York: Crown Publishing Group, 2007.

Freedman-Spizman, Robyn, and Rick Frishman. *Where's Your WOW?: 16 Ways to Make Your Competitors Wish They Were You!* Columbus: McGraw-Hill, 2008.

Friedmann, Susan. *Riches in Niches: How to Make It Big in a Small Market.* Franklin Lakes, N.J.: Career Press, 2007.

Frishman, Rick. *Guerilla Publicity: Getting Gobs of Media Coverage Without Spending Lots of Money or Time.* Newark: *Audible.com* (download).

Frishman, Rick, and Robyn Freedman-Spizman. *Author 101 Bestselling Book Proposals: The Insider's Guide to Selling Your Work (Author 101).* Cincinnati: Adams Media Corporation, 2005.

Frishman, Rick, Jill Lublin, and Mark Steisel. *Networking Magic: Find the Best—from Doctors, Lawyers, and Accountants to Homes, Schools, and Jobs.* Cincinnati: Adams Media Corporation, 2004.

Frishman, Rick, Robyn Freedman-Spizman, and Mark Steisel. *Author 101 Bestselling Book Publicity: The Insider's Guide to Promoting Your Book—and Yourself.* Cincinnati: Adams Media Corporation, 2006.

Gerber, Michael E. *The E-Myth Revisited: Why Most Small Businesses Don't Work and What to Do About It.* New York: HarperCollins Publishers, 1995.

Gladwell, Malcolm. *Blink: The Power of Thinking Without Thinking.* New York: Little, Brown and Company, 2005.

——. *The Tipping Point: How Little Things Can Make a Big Difference.* New York: Back Bay Books , 2002.

Godin, Seth. *All Marketers Are Liars: The Power of Telling Authentic Stories in a Low-Trust World.* New York: Portfolio Hardcover, 2005.

——. *The Dip: A Little Book That Teaches You When to Quit (and When to Stick).* New York: Portfolio Hardcover, 2007.

——. *Meatball Sundae: Is Your Marketing out of Sync?* New York: Portfolio Hardcover, 2007.

——. *Permission Marketing.* New York: Simon & Schuster, 1999.

——. *Purple Cow: Transform Your Business by Being Remarkable.* New York: Portfolio Hardcover, 2003.

——. *Small Is the New Big: and 183 Other Riffs, Rants, and Remarkable Business Ideas.* New York: Portfolio Hardcover, 2006.

Goleman, Daniel. *Vital Lies, Simple Truths: The Psychology of Self Deception.* New York: Simon & Schuster, 1996.

Gossage, Howard Luck. *The Book of Gossage.* Chicago: The Copy Workshop, 1995.

Greene, Robert. *The Art of Seduction.* New York: Penguin (Non-Classics), 2003.

——. *The 48 Laws of Power.* New York: Penguin (Non-Classics), 2000.

Gulledge, Andrew K. *The Art of Persuasion: A Practical Guide to Improving Your Convincing Power.* Lincoln, Neb.: iUniverse, 2004.

Heath, Chip, and Dan Heath. *Made to Stick: Why Some Ideas Survive and Others Die.* New York: Random House, 2007.

Heinrichs, Jay. *Thank You for Arguing: What Aristotle, Lincoln, and Homer Simpson Can Teach Us About the Art of Persuasion.* New York: Three Rivers Press, 2007.

Hill, Napoleon. *Think and Grow Rich.* New York: Ballantine Books, 1996.

Hogan, Kevin. *The Psychology of Persuasion: How to Persuade Others to Your Way of Thinking.* Gretna, La.: Pelican Publishing Company, 1996.

——. *The Science of Influence: How to Get Anyone to Say "Yes" in 8 Minutes or Less!* Hoboken, N.J.: Wiley, 2004.

——. *Talk Your Way to the Top: Communication Secrets to Change Your Life.* Gretna, La.: Pelican Publishing Company, 1999.

Hogan, Kevin, and James Speakman. Covert Persuasion: Psychological Tactics and Tricks to Win the Game. Hoboken, N.J.: Wiley, 2006.

Hopkins, Claude C. *Scientific Advertising.* La Vergne, Tenn.: FQ Classics/Filiquarian Publishing, LLC, 2007.

Horowitz, Shel. *Ethics in Marketing.* Mumbai, India: Jaico Publishing House, 2006.

——. *Grassroots Marketing for Authors and Publishers.* West Conshohocken, Pa.: Infinity Publishing, 2007.

——. *Grassroots Marketing: Getting Noticed in a Noisy World.* White River Jct., Vt.: Chelsea Green Publishing Company, 2000.

——. *Principled Profit: Marketing That Puts People First.* Hadley, Mass.: Accurate Writing & More, 2003.

Jantsch, John. *Duct Tape Marketing: The World's Most Practical Small Business Marketing Guide.* Nashville: Thomas Nelson, 2007.

Johnson, Spencer. *Who Moved My Cheese?* London: Ebury Press, 2002.

Joyner, Mark. *The Great Formula: for Creating Maximum Profit with Minimal Effort.* Hoboken, N.J.: Wiley, 2006.

———. *The Irresistible Offer: How to Sell Your Product or Service in 3 Seconds or Less.* Hoboken, N.J.: Wiley, 2005.

———. *MindControlMarketing.com: How Everyday People are Using Forbidden Mind Control Psychology and Ruthless Military Tactics to Make Millions Online.* Auckland, New Zealand: Steel Icarus Books, 2002.

———. *Simpleology: The Simple Science of Getting What You Want.* Hoboken, N.J.: Wiley, 2007.

Kennedy, Dan S. *How to Make Millions with Your Ideas: An Entrepreneur's Guide.* New York: Plume, 1996.

King, Stephen. *On Writing.* New York: Scribner, 2000.

Klaus, Peggy. *Brag!: The Art of Tooting Your Own Horn without Blowing It.* New York: Warner Business Books, 2004.

Knowles, Eric S., and Jay A. Linn. *Resistance and Persuasion.* Philadelphia: Lawrence Erlbaum, 2003.

Kremer, John. *1001 Ways to Market Your Books (For Authors and Publishers), Sixth Edition.* Taos, N.Mex.: Open Horizons, 2006.

Kunde, Jesper. *Corporate Religion: Building a Strong Company Through Personality and Corporate Soul.* Essex, UK: Financial Times/Prentice Hall, 2000.

Lakhani, Dave. *Persuasion: The Art of Getting What You Want.* Hoboken, N.J.: Wiley, 2005.

———. *Power of An Hour: Business and Life Mastery in One Hour a Week.* Hoboken, N.J.: Wiley, 2006.

———. *Subliminal Persuasion: Influence & Marketing Secrets They Don't Want You To Know.* Hoboken, N.J.: Wiley, 2008.

Levine, Robert V. *The Power of Persuasion: How We're Bought and Sold.* Hoboken, N.J.: Wiley, 2006.

Levinson, Jay Conrad. *Guerrilla Advertising.* Boston: Houghton Mifflin, 1994.

———. *Guerrilla Marketing, 4th Edition: Easy and Inexpensive Strategies for Making Big Profits from Your Small Business.* Boston: Houghton Mifflin, 2007.

Levinson, Jay Conrad, Rick Frishman, and Jill Lublin. *Guerrilla Publicity: Hundreds of Sure-Fire Tactics to Get Maximum Sales for Minimum Dollars.* Cincinnati: Adams Media Corporation, 2002.

Levitin, Daniel J. *This Is Your Brain on Music: The Science of a Human Obsession.* New York: Dutton Adult, 2006.

Levitt, Steven D., and Stephen J. Dubner. *Freakonomics: A Rogue Economist Explores the Hidden Side of Everything.* New York: William Morrow, 2006.

Lynch, Aaron. *Thought Contagion.* New York: Basic Books, 1998.

Mack, Ben. *Think Two Products Ahead: Secrets the Big Advertising Agencies Don't Want You to Know and How to Use Them for Bigger Profits.* Hoboken, N.J.: Wiley, 2007.

McKenna, Regis. *The Regis Touch: New Marketing Strategies for Uncertain Times.* CITY TK: Addison Wesley, 1985.

Messaris, Paul. *Visual Persuasion: The Role of Images in Advertising.* Thousand Oaks, Calif.: SAGE Publications, 1996.

Micek, John-Paul, and Deborah Micek. *Secrets of Online Persuasion: Captivating the Hearts, Minds and Pocketbooks of Thousands Using Blogs, Podcasts and Other New Media Marketing Tools.* Garden City, N.Y.: Morgan James Publishing, 2006.

Mortensen, Kurt W., and Robert G. Allen. *Maximum Influence: The 12 Universal Laws of Power Persuasion.* New York: AMACOM, 2004.

Neumeier, Marty. *The Brand Gap: Expanded Edition.* Berkeley, Calif.: Peachpit Press, 2005.

Ogilvy, David. *Confessions of an Advertising Man.* London: Southbank Pub., 2004.

———. *Ogilvy on Advertising.* New York: Vintage, 1985.

Packard, Vance Oakley. *The Hidden Persuaders.* Brooklyn: Ig Publishing, 2007.

Patterson, Kerry, Joseph Grenny, David Maxfield, Ron McMillan, and Al Switzler. *Influencer: The Power to Change Anything.* New York: McGraw-Hill, 2007.

Port, Michael. *Book Yourself Solid: The Fastest, Easiest, and Most Reliable System for Getting More Clients Than You Can Handle Even if You Hate Marketing and Selling*. Hoboken, N.J.: Wiley, 2006.

Puhn, Laurie. *Instant Persuasion*. New York: Tarcher, 2006.

Rapaille, Clotaire. *The Culture Code: An Ingenious Way to Understand Why People Around the World Live and Buy as They Do*. New York: Broadway, 2007.

Ries, Al, and Jack Trout. *The 22 Immutable Laws of Marketing: Violate Them at Your Own Risk!* New York: HarperBusiness, 1994.

Robbins, Mike. *Focus on the Good Stuff: The Power of Appreciation*. San Francisco: Jossey-Bass, 2007.

Rosen, Emanuel. *The Anatomy of Buzz: How to Create Word of Mouth Marketing*. New York: Doubleday Publishing, 2002.

Rushkoff, Douglas. *Coercion*. New York: Audio Renaissance, 1999.

Sagmeister, Stefan. *Things I Have Learned in My Life So Far*. New York: Harry N. Abrams/HNA Books, 2008.

Schwartz, David. *The Magic of Thinking Big*. New York: Fireside Group (Simon & Schuster), 1987.

Sernovitz, Andy. *Word of Mouth Marketing: How Smart Companies Get People Talking*. New York: Kaplan Business, 2006.

Steel, Jon. *Truth, Lies and Advertising: The Art of Account Planning*. Hoboken, N.J.: Wiley, 1998.

Sullivan, Luke. *Hey, Whipple, Squeeze This: A Guide to Creating Great Ads, Second Edition*. Hoboken, N.J.: Wiley, 2003.

Taleb, Nassim Nicholas. *The Black Swan: The Impact of the Highly Improbable*. New York: Random House, 2007.

——. *Fooled by Randomness: The Hidden Role of Chance in Life and in the Markets*. New York: Random House Trade Paperbacks, 2005.

Vitale, Joe. *There's a Customer Born Every Minute: P.T. Barnum's Secrets to Business Success*. New York: AMACOM, 1998.

Vitale, Joe, and Bill Hibbler. *Meet and Grow Rich: How to Easily Create and Operate Your Own "Mastermind" Group for Health, Wealth, and More*. Hoboken, N.J.: Wiley, 2006.

Woodward, Gary C., and Robert E. Denton, Jr. *Persuasion and Influence in American Life*. Long Grove, Ill.: Waveland Press, 2004.

Yudkin, Marcia. *6 Steps to Free Publicity: For Corporate Publicists or Solo Professionals, Including...Publishers, Consultants, Conference Planners, Politicians, Inventors*. Franklin Lakes, N.J.: Career Press, 2003.

Index

About the Author

Ken McArthur knows how to create impact. He built his marketing career on the philosophy that partnerships and collaboration build value for everyone.

By coaching and mentoring people who want to make a difference—in addition to creating books, home study courses, Websites, and events that foster joint ventures and cooperative efforts—Ken developed a loyal following that includes hundreds of thousands of people trying to make a difference in a noisy world.

Ken's first membership site generated a quarter-million dollars in sales in the first six months, and his second was ranked number 362 out of all of the millions of sites on the Internet in its first day of pre-launch. The members of Ken's *jvAlert.com* Website alone have more than 5 million active subscribers on their combined mailing lists.

To prove that he could generate buzz and create impact, Ken mentored newcomer Sterling Valentine as a demonstration that his system would work. Sterling was a complete unknown with no list, no product, and no partners, who, with Ken's help, created an information product, gathered joint venture partners, created a massive publicity campaign from scratch, and sold $101,153 in just 92 days—all because of the principles that Ken shares in this book.

Ken produced the "bible" of product creation resource packages—a huge collection of DVDs, CDs, and a 673-page workbook called *Info Product Blueprint,* which sold out the complete first production run in less than 48 hours. Sterling Valentine describes *Info Product Blueprint* as a "complete Internet Marketing Encyclopedia."

Regularly asked to speak at leading Internet marketing events and workshops internationally, Ken personally hosts a series of live events that are held three times a year that bring hundreds of top-level marketers together to create joint venture relationships, and create and promote information products.

From the beginning, *jvAlert Live* has been like no other Internet marketing conference. What started as an idea for a casual get-together of Internet marketing friends has grown into a dynamic event, combining top speakers, hot seats, and unparalleled networking opportunities. Above all is the spirit of collaboration that infuses every *jvAlert Live*, leading to many lasting friendships and profitable partnerships.

Ken is also the creator of *AffiliateShowcase.com,* an affiliate program search engine with more than 42,000 Websites currently in its network, and the MBS Internet Research Center, conducting large scale marketing surveys, including the largest survey report ever produced on information products.

Ken writes for multiple high-traffic blogs including *Ken McArthur's Marketing Thoughts* and *The Impact Factor,* and is currently working on *BeyondOneLife.com,* which is a bold new experiment to measure the ways that we make a difference and to show that impact in a powerful way that will encourage you to grow your impact beyond one life.